LAND GIRLS
AND
THEIR IMPACT

LAND GIRLS
AND THEIR
IMPACT

by
ANN KRAMER

First published in Great Britain in 2008
Reprinted in this format in 2009 by
Remember When
An imprint of
Pen & Sword Books Ltd
47 Church Street
Barnsley
South Yorkshire
S70 2AS

Copyright © Ann Kramer 2008, 2009

ISBN 978 184468 091 7

A CIP catalogue record for this book is
available from the British Library

Typeset in Palatino Linotype and Bernhard Modern by
Lamorna Publishing Services

Printed and bound in England
by the MPG Books Group

Pen & Sword Books Ltd incorporates the Imprints of Pen & Sword Aviation,
Pen & Sword Family History, Pen & Sword Maritime, Pen & Sword Military,
Wharncliffe Local History,
Pen & Sword Select, Pen & Sword Military Classics, Leo Cooper,
Remember When, Seaforth Publishing and Frontline Publishing

For a complete list of Pen & Sword titles please contact
PEN & SWORD BOOKS LIMITED
47 Church Street, Barnsley, South Yorkshire, S70 2AS, England
E-mail: enquiries@pen-and-sword.co.uk
Website: www.pen-and-sword.co.uk

This book is dedicated to Phyllis, Helen, Margaret, Eileen, Hazel, Blanche, Joan, Beryl, Peggy, Stella, Pamela, Sheelah and all former members of the Women's Land Army

Contents

Acknowledgements . . . .*ix*
Permissions . . . .*x*
Timeline . . . .*xi*
Interviewees . . . .*xvii*
Introduction . . . .*xix*

Chapter 1 First Time Around 1
Chapter 2 War Returns 10
Chapter 3 Recruitment and Propaganda 24
Chapter 4 Who Were the Land Girls? 42
Chapter 5 Working on the Land .58
Chapter 6 The Lumber Jills 80
Chapter 7 Living with Others 96
Chapter 8 Acceptance and Prejudice 119
Chapter 9 Love, Sex and Romance 134
Chapter 10 End of War 149
Chapter 11 Reflections 166

Bibliography *178*
Index *180*

Acknowledgements

Thanks are due to the following:

The Imperial War Museum for permission to use extracts from *Meet the Members: A Record of the Timber Corps of the Women's Land Army; The Women's Land Army* by Vita Sackville-West; and *An Anthology of Verse* by members of the Women's Land Army. All three have been reprinted by the Imperial War Museum as part of their Women at War Series

Brenzett Aeronautical Museum, and Ray Brignall, for permission to take and use photographs of exhibits in the Museum.

Former members of the Women's Land Army, who gave me permission to use extracts from personal interviews and to reproduce photographs and memorabilia They are named in the introduction to the book.

Pamela McDowell for permission to use extracts from her private papers, *Memories of the Women's Land Army in Kent 1944-45*, held in the Imperial War Museum, Documents Department

Sutton Publishing for permission to quote from Annice Gibbs' account in *Women at War 1939-1945 The Home Front* by Carol Harris, published in 2000.

The Random House Group Ltd. for permission to quote from 'The Rewards of Hard Labour' by Pat Parker, taken from *What Did You Do in the War, Mummy?* by Mavis Nicholson, published by Chatto & Windus, 1995.

Permissions

I would like to thank the following or their families for kindly providing the illustrations for this book:

Sheelah Cruttenden – Images 5-6, 17-18, 39

Helen Dawson (née Buss) – Images 40, 38, 42, 4a-6a, 8a

Eileen Grabham (née Styles) – Images 10-12, 31

Betty Hamer (née Towse) – Image 27

Eileen Hodd (née Jarman) – Images 33-35

Hazel King (née Bannister) – Images 13-14, 19-22, 25, 28, 2a-3a, 7a, 10a, 12a-13a

Blanche Lucas – Image 14a

Joan Markby (née Moody) – Images 8-9, 26, 32

Peggy Pearce – Images 15-16, 23-24, 29-30, 36-37, 9a

I would also like to thank St. Clements Church, Old Town Hastings for allowing me to take photographs there.

Timeline

1917

Women's Land Army is formed under the directorship of Dame Meriel Talbot. Some 23,000 women are recruited to work on the land.

1918

British women over the age of 30 gain the vote; women over 21 can be Members of Parliament.

1919

First Women's Land Army is disbanded.

1928

British women over 21 have the vote on equal basis with men.

1938

German troops march into Czechoslovakia. British government plans for war. Gas masks are distributed to British population.

April: Women's Voluntary Service (WVS) is formed, with just five members. By 1941 membership has grown to more than 1 million.
Ministry of Agriculture approach Lady Denman with a request to reform the Women's Land Army. Lady Denman draws up

plans for countrywide organization and recruitment but there are delays in implementing her proposals.

1939

June – September: Three and a half million British people, mainly children, evacuated from the cities.

1 June: Women's Land Army is re-formed with Lady Gertrude Denman as Honorary Director. County and regional officers are appointed. Recruitment begins in earnest for Land Army members, known popularly as 'land girls'.

29 August: Lady Denman sets up the Women's Land Army headquarters at her home at Balcombe Place, Sussex.

1 September: Germany invades Poland

3 September: Britain, its empire and France declare war on Germany. The Second World War begins. About 1.5 million British people, mainly children, are evacuated to the country-side.

December: some 4,500 land girls are employed on the land, working through one of the most bitter winters recorded.

1940

January: Food rationing begins in Britain: butter, ham, bacon, tea, meat, eggs, cheese and sugar are the first foods to be rationed.

April: Women's Land Army begins publishing the *Land Girl*, a monthly magazine with Mrs Margaret Pyke as editor. Its aim is to keep land girls in touch with each other. Circulation eventually reaches over 21,000 copies.

May: Germany invades Low Countries; Home Guard formed in Britain.

June: German troops invade Paris; fall of France.

June: About 6,000 land girls now employed on farms in Britain.

August – September: Battle of Britain.

September: Start of the Blitz. Germany bombs British cities.

1941

May: All British women aged between 19 – 40 have to register at labour exchanges for war work.

June: Clothes rationing begins, Britain. Germany invades Russia.

June: Fourteen thousand members of the Women's Land Army now employed on the land.

December: In Britain Churchill's wartime government passes the National Service Act (No. 2), allowing for the conscription of women. All unmarried women between the ages of 20 – 30 were called up for war work. This is later extended to include women aged up to 43 and married women. Pregnant women and those with children could be exempt.

December: Japanese bomb Pearl Harbor, Hawaii. The United States enters the war on Allied side.

1942

January: American GIs arrive in Britain.

March: The Women's Timber Corps is formed in Britain. More than 4,000 women, known popularly as 'lumberjills' are employed in forestry during the war years.

June: Some 40,000 land girls now employed on the land. Lady Denman starts Lady Army's Benevolent Fund to provide financial assistance for land girls in difficulties.

3 July: Queen Elizabeth hosts a 3rd birthday party for the Women's Land Army.

27 July: Australian Women's Land Army formed. By 1943 there

are 2,382 permanent members and 1,039 auxiliary members.

December: American First Lady, Mrs Eleanor Roosevelt, meets Land Army members during her visit to the UK.

1943

In Britain, nine out of ten single women and eight out of ten married women are either in the forces, the Land Army or in war industries.

American Women's Land Army is formed and continues until 1947. It recruits more than 1 million members.

January: German army surrenders at Stalingrad

March – September: Allies bomb Germany. Fuel and food shortages in all warring countries.

June: About 65,000 women are now serving in the Women's Land Army. They are producing 70 per cent of Britain's food.

October: Between 70 – 90 per cent of British women engaged in war work of some sort.

December: More than 80,000 women are employed in the Land Army. Government has ended recruitment although women are still keen to join. Recruitment will begin again in 1944/45 when it becomes clear that the Land Army will still be needed after the war.

1944

May: Women's Land Army headquarters moves back to London but returns to Sussex after doodlebug attacks begin.

June: Allied forces land in France (D-Day landings) The first German VI bomb (doodlebug) hits Britain.

August: Allies liberate Paris.

September: V2 attacks.

1945

February: Allied air attacks devastate Dresden, Germany.

16 February: Lady Denman resigns as director of the Women's Land Army in protest at the Government's decision to exclude members of the Women's Land Army from post-war financial benefits.

14 April: About 150 land girls in North Gloucester call a one-day strike in protest against Government's decision not to grant post-war gratuities to land girls.

7 May: Germany surrenders; 8 May VE (Victory in Europe) Day.

6 and 9 August: Allies drop atomic bombs on Hiroshima and Nagasaki, Japan.

14 August: Japan surrenders. Second World War ends.

15 August: VJ day celebrated.

7 December: Queen presents golden armbands to long serving land girls.

31 December: Australian Women's Land Army disbanded.

1946

8 June: Land Army marches in Victory Parade, London.

August: Numbers of Women's Land Army now about 54,000.

August: Some 750 land girls march through City of London to receive armlets from the Queen.

31 August: Women's Timber Corps disbanded.

1947

March: The *Land Girl* magazine ceases publication. A free newsletter from headquarters, the *Land Army News,* replaces the magazine and continues until 1950.

1948

Land Army County Committees are dissolved.

1949

October: Tom Williams, Ministry of Agriculture, announces that the Women's Land Army is to be disbanded.

1950

Some 8,000 women are still in the Land Army.

21 October: Women's Land Army disbanded. Five hundred land girls march past Buckingham Palace, London, in the stand-down parade.

1995

19 August: Eighty former land girls wearing Land Army armbands march through London as part of the 50th anniversary of VJ Day.

2000

November: Women's Land Army is finally invited to the Remembrance Day march past at the Cenotaph, London.

2007

October: First memorial to the Women's Timber Corps is unveiled in Scotland. Former members of the Women's Land Army continue campaigning for veteran's medal.

2008

January: Former members of the Women's Land Army and Women's Timber Corps can apply for a special badge commemorating their work during the Second World War.

Interviewees

The following women kindly gave interviews or provided written pieces for this book. Many also lent photographs and memorabilia.

Phyllis Cole (née Butler) Age 87
  Worked in a mobile threshing gang going to farms in the Uckfield area, Sussex.

Sheelah Cruttenden (née Magan), deceased
  Land Army 1943-1946; 1947-1949. Field work in Gloucester, subsequently Sussex. Memories and recollections provided by her children and from Sheelah's own writing.

Margaret Donaldson (née Irwin) Age 84
  Served nearly two years with the WLA in East Suffolk, mainly milking and working with cows. Left to go into the ATS.

Helen Dawson (née Buss) Age 84
  Land Army 1945-48.
  Dairy and general farming Kent

Eileen Grabham (née Styles) Age 81
  Served in the Land Army 1943-1947.
  Londoner. Field and dairy work, Kent

Eileen Hodd (née Jarman) Age 80
  Land Army 1942/3-1947.
  General farming, fruit picking, harvesting, hop growing, Kent.

Stella Hope (née Standen) Age: not known
Land Army 1946-1950.
General farming, threshing, bailing, harvesting. Cumberland and Kent.

Hazel King (née Bannister) ('Basil') Age 83, deceased 2008
Land Army 1943-1947.
Tractor driving and mixed farming, Kent

Blanche Lucas (née Veness) Age 83
Land Army 1942-1946
Milking, harvesting, Sussex

Joan Markby (née Moody) Age 85
Land Army 1943-1945
Milking, dairy work, mixed farming, Dorset

Eleanor Beryl Peacham (née Cooke) (Known as Beryl) Age 82
Land Army 1943
Dairy work and mixed farming, Kent

Peggy Pearce (née Robertson) Age 90
Land Army 1939-1945
Dairy and mixed farming Bristol area and Surrey

Other former land girls interviewed at Brenzett:

Carole Warner, about her mother, Mrs Betty Hamer
Bernice Winifred Birch, joined Land Army 1940
Rose Hignett ('Little Rose')
Audrey Blythe ('Titch')
Marge, from mid-Wales
June Ivy Merritt, joined Land Army 1947
Daphne Bass
Marjorie Williams

Introduction

An Extraordinary Army

IT WAS a typical British summer day in August: grey skies and teeming rain, and I was standing in a field in Brenzett, Kent. Looking around me it would have been easy to imagine that it was August 1941 rather than August 2007. Two magnificent Shire horses, pulling a plough, circled the field, which was lined with puffing tractors, wartime farming implements, and rows of wartime vehicles from Mercedes through to commercial vans. A replica 1940s shop, complete with wartime tins and packaging, sold fresh vegetables at wartime prices and, standing in the centre of the field surrounded by bales of hay, an old bicycle and basket of vegetables, were two young women, dressed head to toe in the distinctive jodhpurs, brown hats and greenish-khaki jumpers of the WLA. Wartime songs from loudspeakers filled the damp air.

The stars of the day, however, were sixty or so older women who, despite the dreadful weather, arrived in the field for a major event: a WLA reunion that takes place every year at the Brenzett Aeronautical Museum, which is housed in what used to be a WLA hostel that to this day contains a wooden door displaying graffiti left behind by the young land girls who lived there during the war. It is a fascinating place that has been lovingly restored by Ray Brignall, a local farmer and Land Army enthusiast, who spent four years recreating exact plans of the original hostel that are on display today. The museum needs support if it is to survive.

Every year former land girls, particularly those who were based in Kent or Sussex, arrive at Brenzett for this reunion. They assemble in a large marquee, enjoy lunch and make the most of an opportunity to swap stories, meet old friends or colleagues, remember departed friends and generally chat over the recollections of what, for most of them, was the most significant experience of their lives, not just living through a war, but being members of the WLA.

They have every right to do this. During the Second World War, well over 100,000 British women of varying ages and backgrounds worked on the land to replace men who had gone to fight and to help produce the nation's food and timber. More than 80,000 of these women were members of the WLA, who had responded to increasingly urgent calls for agricultural labour, initially to bring in the harvest of 1939 but also to maintain food supplies in war-torn Britain. Many of the women, known popularly as 'land girls', had no previous experience of working on the land. At least a third of them came from London or northern cities and many had never even seen a cow before. They worked long hours, in backbreaking conditions, sometimes labouring in the fields directly underneath bombing raids and dog fights, quite unprotected and frequently diving into hedgerows or ditches to escape falling bombs and scattered shrapnel.

Thanks to the work of the WLA, British people did not starve during the Second World War, unlike their civilian counterparts in occupied Holland and France and in Germany. By 1943, the WLA was providing something like 70 per cent of the nation's food which, together with rationing, meant that the British population were able to eat a balanced and extremely healthy diet throughout the war, even if food dishes were sometimes peculiar and more exotic fruits and foodstuffs were absent. The work of the WLA meant that Germany failed in a major objective, which was to starve Britain into submission

To do this work however the WLA encountered considerable prejudice and discrimination. Lady Gertrude Denman, honorary director of the WLA, had to battle constantly against official foot dragging and a reluctance from officialdom to recognize both the need for, and value of, women's work on the land. Many farmers too, to say nothing of the National Farmers'

Union (NFU), were sometimes at best lukewarm about women land workers and at worst downright prejudiced. Not only did Lady Denman have to face one hurdle after another but also land girls themselves, as is so often the case for women, had to work doubly hard to prove themselves as capable, skilled and essential workers.

Prove themselves they did: eventually farmers and others changed their minds dramatically as the hard work, dedication and abilities of the WLA broke down long-held prejudices and eventually won over male bastions such as the National Farmers Union who, by the end of the war, had become outspoken champions of the WLA, most particularly when it became clear that the WLA were not going to receive the official recognition they deserved.

For, surprisingly, despite its enormous contribution to the British war effort, the WLA has often been described, not least by its own members, as the 'forgotten army' largely because it received very little recognition for its work both at the time and after the war. Although members of the WLA marched in victory parades in 1945 and 1946, the British Government did not invite them to the Cenotaph until 2000 and it was not until December 2007 that the British government announced that surviving members of the WLA would finally receive a special commendation for their work during the Second World War.

It is puzzling to know why this should be so; former members of the WLA have their own opinions, which they are quite prepared to voice, but they are surprisingly lacking in bitterness about the official neglect and recognition for such an extraordinarily dedicated and hardworking labour force. Official reasons are put forward but they are difficult to accept. Maybe it was pure misogyny or maybe it was because work on the land was then, as now, often not very highly regarded. Whatever the reasons, there is little doubt that the Land Army has not, until recently, been as well known or as widely covered as women in other wartime services; it has rarely received the same coverage as other women's war experiences although, interestingly, when I discussed this book with friends, I was amazed by the large number of people who said that their mothers, aunts or grandmothers had served in the Land Army.

What struck me at Brenzett was the strength, determination and liveliness of the women, or self-described 'girls', who had gathered for the reunion that day. Most surviving Land Army members are now well into their eighties, but most remain active and their memories of their land girl experiences are as clear as day, and they obviously take a considerable pleasure in talking about them. Some were surprised that anyone today still wanted to know about the Land Army – in fact, one former land girl joked 'You don't want to know' when I asked her about it – but most believe that it is important that their work is remembered and acknowledged and are thrilled that the interest still exists. They themselves are often somewhat matter of fact about what they did: it was wartime, there was a need, they had a job to do, and that was that. But they were an extraordinary army: they took on a male-dominated world and proved their worth and I am pleased to have had the opportunity to gain a glimpse into their lives.

I am grateful to all the women I met at Brenzett, who shared experiences with me, and would like to make a special thanks to former land girls and adult children of land girls, who not only invited me into their homes and allowed me to interview them but also gave me tea and cakes. It was a joy and privilege to meet them. I would particularly like to thank Phyllis Cole, Helen Dawson, Margaret Donaldson, Eileen Hodd, Hazel King, Blanche Lucas, Joan Markby, Beryl Peacham and Peggy Pearce. I would also like to thank Stella Hope and Blanche Lucas for providing written pieces and Helen Dawson for writing a poem. My thanks also to Lee Jabbit, Jennifer Grist, Paula Barnard and James Cruttenden for sharing memories of their mother, Sheelah Cruttenden, and for permission to quote from her written account. My thanks as well to everyone who lent photographs and memorabilia for use in the book, including Carole Warner who sent me a photograph of her mother, Betty Hamer. I would also like to thank the Imperial War Museum for the help they gave to me: their archives contain the most fascinating material on the WLA; sadly I could only scratch the surface but it was there that I found Pamela McDowell's recollections of her time in the Land Army and I would like to thank her for permission to quote from her papers. Thanks as well to the staff of Hastings Reference Library, who helped me through the vagaries of the microfiche as I ploughed through wartime editions of the *Sussex Express* and finally I would like to thank Ray Brignall for allowing me access to the Brenzett Museum and Phil Wilkinson for tracking down records of the land girls' strike in Cheltenham.

Because I live in Sussex, many of the personal accounts in this book come from former land girls who were based in the southeast, some of whom provided me with more material than I could use. I hope what I have selected meets with their approval and that the information in this book rings true for all former land girls. I have enormous respect for their achievements.

Chapter 1

First Time Around: The origins of the Women's Land Army

*N*O *soldier can now be spared from France. The harvest, which alone can save us from defeat, is in the hands of our women…*

(The *Landswoman*, May 1918)

THE WOMEN'S Land Army, with its distinctive breeches, smocks, boots and cloche hats, made its first appearance during the so-called Great War of 1914-18. It was formed at breakneck speed by upper- and middle-class women who, when war broke out, were among the many British women who threw themselves into organizing women for the war effort, during the process helping to break the mould and open up new opportunities for women.

Origins of the WLA

From the first, the WLA was a voluntary organization and from its outset, to quote *The Times*, it was 'a very remarkable movement that…perhaps more than any of the other services tested the patriotism of its members'.

The early origins of the WLA lay in the Women's Farm and Garden Association, which was created in 1899 by a group of upper-class women with the aim of training and advising women who wanted to take up farming and gardening as a profession. One of the leading lights of the Union was Miss Meriel Talbot (later Dame Meriel Talbot), an inspiring and determined woman who had her own cricket team and delighted in the nickname 'Slasher' Talbot.

When war broke out in 1914, thousands of British men joined

up in a frenzy of patriotic idealism and marched off to the front – many never returned. Women such as leading suffragette Emmeline Pankhurst, who had been locked in battle with an obstinate government that refused to give votes for women, now put their suffrage demands on hold, demanded the 'right to serve' and directed their energies into organizing women for the war effort. This stand did, in fact, split the women's suffrage movement, as there were other activists, such as Sylvia Pankhurst, who opposed the war. A host of voluntary organizations sprang up, most led by women of independent means who were inspired by a patriotic wish to help their country and provide support in all areas from policing through to nursing and caring for the troops. Miss Meriel Talbot and her colleagues focused on the need for women land workers.

In Britain at that time only about 117,000 women worked on the land: they were employed in dairies and on seasonal work such as fruit and hop picking but in general, and in sharp contrast to mainland Europe where it was traditional for women to work on the land, the hard labour of farming was not seen as women's work – it was the preserve of men. Resistance to bringing in women land workers was widespread: most British farmers and indeed villagers were highly prejudiced against using women, particularly women from cities and towns, believing that such women were too delicate for farm work and would not be able to 'stick' the rigours of agricultural life. Instead, as farm workers left the land in droves, farmers called on men who were too old to enlist or used skilled farm workers, who were released temporarily from the army to help with harvesting and other seasonal work.

Appeals for Women Land Workers

By autumn 1915, some 300,000 male agricultural workers had left the land to fight and the need for more workers was becoming pressing. Britain relied heavily on imported foodstuffs: the country produced only about one-third of its food, and German attacks on shipping were intensifying. It was essential to increase home grown reserves of food. Despite deep-rooted prejudice on the part of farmers, it was clear that women were needed. Voluntary organizations such as the Women's Legion and the Women's Defence Relief Corps, working with the government through the War Agricultural Committees of the Board of Trade, began more intensive recruitment drives to persuade women to offer their services on the land – and to persuade farmers to accept them. Under Miss Talbot's leadership, the Women's Farm and Garden Union set up a system of training farms both to equip women with farming skills and to persuade farmers of the value of women's work.

> Some people tell me that I shall not be able to go on with my farm work in the winter, because it will make my hands so bad. But I intend to stick to it. Our men don't stop fighting in the cold weather, and neither shall I. My only brother is in the trenches...
> (Miss Dorothy Chalmers, 1915)

Appeals were circulated for women land workers so that men could be released for fighting but there were many barriers to overcome: farmers' prejudice, the isolation and difficulties of farm work, its lack of glamour and the fact that munitions work and other services were taking up most resources. Patriotism was often used as a rallying call. In 1916 the *Daily News and Leader* reflected these issues, and prevailing views of women, in its Appeal for Women Land Workers:

Already the country has raised an Army, say, 4,000,000 men for the front. It has organised another army...of 250,000 women for munitions factories. There now remains the problem of mobilising yet another army of 400,000 women for the land...the most difficult problem of all. Work on the land is not popular...No woman can be expected to enjoy milking cows at four on a winter morning, or spreading manure, or cleaning a pigsty...much of the most necessary work is hard unpleasant, and by no means extravagantly paid. This is why the appeal is made exclusively to the patriotism of women... .

Despite these barriers, however, women were responding, coming forward, receiving training and being placed on farms. Gradually some were being issued with uniform style working clothes to highlight their situation as war workers. Women from cities and towns began taking up tasks such as milking, planting, fruit picking and hoeing and the first signs of a formal Land Army uniform appeared as women land workers were issued with lace-up boots, smocks and breeches.

In 1916 with the help of a government grant, the Women's National Land Service Corps was launched under Mrs Rowland

> ...Our beds are just off the floor on a wooden frame, a straw mattress and pillow and five blankets...The camp is miles from anywhere, absolutely isolated...The snow was too thick to work so we carried wood from the piling stations and sawed it for indoor use...We have breakfast at 6.30 and another at 9.30...After lunch we went to the woods and started our new work. It is great axing at great trees. We were given a billhook, an axe, a saw and a cord measure...Today has been grand. Very cold but the work is fine. It is great to watch a grand old tree crash to the earth and feel that you did it alone – Life is just what I have always longed for...
>
> (Miss B. Bennett, Women's Timber Corps, 1916)

Williams. It was an offshoot of the Women's Farm and Garden Association and came into being with the explicit aim of 'speeding up the recruiting of all classes of women for work on the land in order to ensure the maintenance of home-grown food supply'. Working under the auspices of the Board of Agriculture and funded by it, the Land Corps organized supplies of temporary war workers for seasonal jobs such as harvesting, fruit picking and potato lifting. It dealt with providing emergency war work on the land, recruiting part-time workers and organizing gangs of village women. That year too and recognizing her undoubted experience and skills, the Ministry of Agriculture appointed Miss Talbot to advise them on how best to encourage women 'to come forward from their villages, homes and elsewhere to help the farmers'.

The First Women's Land Army

By 1917 Britain was in dire straits. Mounting casualties meant even more men were leaving the land, the harvest failed and German U-boats had completely interrupted imports.

According to some accounts there was only about three weeks' food supply left in the country. The need for a large and steady supply of women workers was critical and recruiting appeals stressed the urgency. Following a delegation from the Land Corp, Mr Prothero, then president of the Board of Agriculture, took an unprecedented step: he formed a Women's Branch of the Board of Agriculture that was staffed exclusively by women and Miss Meriel Talbot was appointed to co-ordinate the recruitment, training and placing of women land workers. Paid women officers were appointed in each county and in early 1917 the WLA was officially launched with Miss Meriel Talbot as director. Writing about that time in the WLA manual during the Second World War, Dame Meriel Talbot remembered that:

> ...1917 was a sombre year for our country. I recall Mr Prothero's saying at that time "England is like a beleaguered city". There was only about three weeks' food supply in the country. The need for a mobile force of women to supplement the part-time workers, to go anywhere and give their help where and when it was wanted became apparent – thus the WLA came into being in 1917...

Interestingly, one of the women officials who worked closely with Dame Meriel Talbot during the First World War was Lady Gertrude Denman who, twenty years later, would re-establish the WLA to meet the demands of a second global war.

Now finally in existence, the WLA moved fast. It was highly efficient. Women's Agricultural Committees were appointed in each county; county offices were opened and organizing secretaries were appointed. Women inspectors travelled around supervising work in their areas, while group leaders oversaw work in the villages. Different sections were set up to deal with matters such as training, hostels, equipment, and recruitment.

Recruitment was intensive: work in the Land Army was not as glamorous as work in the other women's services, such as the newly formed Women's Air Force (WAAF), or Women's Royal Naval Services (WRNS), which were created in 1917, so the appeal from the government and officers of the WLA was to patriotism. The emphasis was on freeing men for France, and bringing in the harvest. In 1918 Prime Minister David Lloyd George added his voice to the appeal, telling women that, '...the harvest is in danger...once again therefore...I appeal to women to come forward and help. They have never failed this country yet...' (The *Landswoman*, June 1918)

Members of the Land Army themselves also threw their energies into recruitment, with rallies and processions that helped to publicize the organization and encourage others to join. In March 1918, *The Times* reported on a recruiting campaign for 12,000 women that took place in London, and culminated in a visit to Buckingham Palace by 130 land girls, including tractor drivers, dairywomen, forestry workers and forage girls, some of whom had come from as far as Wales to recruit for the Land Army. The article described how the land girls, having been given lunch at the Savoy, circulated among city workers, carrying banners exhorting town women to join the Land Army and made speeches from hay wagons before being inspected by the Queen at Buckingham Palace. According to the article, 'the health and happiness, clear skins and bright eyes' as well as the enthusiasm of the land girls was strong propaganda.

Recruits

Thousands of women responded to the appeals. In all some 45,000 women applied for work with the WLA, many of them upper- or middle-class young women, such as Kathleen Hale, who having studied art at Reading University, went into the Ministry for Food and then joined the Land Army. Interestingly many of the new recruits were attracted to the uniform, as well as being motivated by a wish to serve their country. Some were also keen to leave home and to work in the fresh air. About half were rejected either because they were not considered physically strong enough for the work or because it was feared they would not stick to the work, but ultimately at least 23,000 women were enrolled into the WLA. Their efforts, commitment and hard work finally overcame male prejudice, farmers seeing for themselves just how hard the women worked.

During the relatively short time the first WLA was in existence it set up a countrywide network of organizers and committees and recruited, trained and placed literally thousands of women on the land. The WLA also produced its own journal, the *Landswoman*, to bolster morale and keep 'land girls', as they became known, in touch with each other.

Recruits came from all social classes although most of the land girls were middle-class. They were issued with a distinctive uniform, given training if necessary and paid 18/- a week, later raised to 20/- and 22/-. They worked on just about every farming task from milking through to fruit picking, harvesting, poultry farming and working with pigs. Women drove tractors, worked as farriers, training with local blacksmiths, and by the summer of 1918 were also being trained as thatchers and threshers. Some women worked for the Women's Forestry Corps, a sub-section of the WLA, which was also set up in 1917. These women did valuable work felling and sawing timber for pit props, trench poles, railway sleepers and paper. For many women it was their first experience of country life and of farming and early recruits were the source of jokes and low expectations: The *Landswoman* was full of the difficulties, confusions and mistakes caused by unfamiliar work, albeit presented with great humour and good nature, as well as references to slightly distorted public perceptions. One joke featured in the *Landswoman*, involved three small boys speaking to each other. One boy said 'Why, it's a man!' To this the second boy replied, 'Nor it ain't, it's a woman.' The third boy, however, commented, 'It ain't neither, it's a land worker!' However, despite the ridicule and the unfamiliarity of the work, members of the Land Army adapted quickly and were soon proving their worth.

Taking a Pride

While the WLA always remained a voluntary and civilian organization – in fact it was often felt that military-style discipline would be impossible to impose on land girls – recruits were nevertheless expected to take a pride in their appearance and a conscientious approach to their work. Few women in those days wore trousers – it was considered either daring or shocking – and there were many observers who feared that once women started dressing in trousers, nothing would ever be the same. Through the columns of the *Landswoman*, land girls were exhorted to remember their position and to take a pride in themselves. The message was that each individual land girl represented the Land Army; she had a duty to dress and present herself in an appropriate way. Just because she was wearing trousers, she need not abandon her femininity although she should conduct herself appropriately at work. There were snippets of advice in the *Landswoman* on how to maintain a feminine but dignified appearance and many references to the need to wear hats correctly, an issue that would surface again in the Second World War. Interestingly, the *Landswoman* also speculated on what long-term impact the Land Army might have on womanhood and the British people generally. Recognizing that the immediate purpose of the Land Army was to 'save the freedom of Great Britain by defending these islands against the German attempt to starve us...' the magazine also considered that 'the Land Army may be the pioneer of a newer and a far higher civilization for the British race' by drawing women 'from the toy-like life of our urban civilization' and giving them 'the sense of a larger freedom and a more dignified self-respect', an interesting observation in 1918 and one that was probably also held by women such as Dame Meriel Talbot and Gertrude Denman.

> ...When war mobilised the world, Englishwomen locked up their rainbow coloured wardrobes and put on the liveries of toil.
>
> (The *Landswoman*, November 1918)

Corduroys Defeat German Threat

By the time the war ended in 1918 farmers' scepticism had been overcome and references to land girls usually caused loud cheers from farmers. In 1918 members of the WLA with munitions workers marched through London to the sound of cheering crowds and in November 1918, the *Landswoman* confirmed the achievements of the WLA, stating proudly that, 'the Land Army corduroys have defeated the German threat of starvation'. *The Times*, in its history of the Great War, stated that members of the Land Army were the worst paid of all the women who took up war work, and had in many instances the worst conditions, experiencing 'much loneliness on isolated farms…Yet they were second to no other women's services in their zeal for the honour of their Army, and they adopted in

The following figures from a survey of 12,639 women land workers in 1918, shows the different types of agricultural work that women were doing:

Milkers	5,734	Bailiffs	3
Ploughwomen	260	Threshers	101
Carters	635	Field workers	3,971
Thatchers	84	Market gardeners	515
Shepherds	21	Private gardeners	260
Tractor drivers	293	Other branches	653

their isolated farms a self-discipline that enabled them to uphold the honour of their corps and to break down the former prejudices against them.'

The WLA was disbanded in 1919, having proved at that stage that women were just as capable, if not more so, of doing hard graft on the land. With demobilization, land girls, like other women wartime workers were persuaded back into their homes to relinquish work for returning soldiers. Within 20 years, however, the WLA would be needed again. Unfortunately, many of the problems that dogged its formation first time around would be encountered once more.

Chapter 2

War Returns: The Land Army Reformed

The Land Army fights in the fields. It is in the fields of Britain that the most critical battle of the war may well be fought and won.
(Lady Denman, 1941, foreword to Land Army Manual)

ONLY twenty years after the end of the First World War, it was clear that war was about to erupt once more. During the 1930s fascist dictatorships were established in Italy, Spain and Germany and by the summer of 1938, despite Chamberlain's attempts at appeasement, the British government was planning for war with Nazi Germany. There were few illusions about what such a war might mean: the Spanish Civil War had demonstrated clearly the devastating effects of aerial bombardment and the Government knew that civilians as well as soldiers would be involved.

Farming on the Eve of War

Maintaining adequate food supplies and keeping the population fed during wartime were major concerns. As early as 1936 Sir William Beveridge, who had worked with the Ministry of Food during the First World War and drafted plans for food rationing, had been appointed to chair a sub-committee to 'plan food supplies in time of war'. The British government had no wish to repeat the situation of near starvation that had threatened the country in 1917 and, building on that experience, knew that farming and the production of home-grown food would be one of the key elements in surviving this coming war.

However, British farming, on the eve of war, was in a sorry state. Unlike Germany, which produced four-fifths of its food, Britain imported at least 70 per cent of all the nation's food. Nearly 70 per cent of cereals and fats came from abroad, as did 70 per cent of its cheese and sugar, nearly 80 per cent of its fruit, and about half of all meat. Most animal foodstuff was also imported. British farming had done well during the First World War when it was vital to produce more food – nearly 2 million acres of grassland had been ploughed up for wheat – but once war had ended, agricultural land was either turned over to pasture or left untended. By 1931, the acreage under wheat was the lowest ever recorded.

Labour too was in short supply. More than one-third of agricultural workers had left the land for work in cities, leaving a shortfall of at least 50,000 agricultural workers. Although in 1924 the government, through the Agricultural Wages Act, had established wage boards to set rates of pay, to enable higher wages for farm labourers, this had also contributed to the drain from the land, as farmers turned to less labour-intensive processes and dismissed workers. State aid increased during the 1930s and marketing boards were introduced to control prices and ensure distribution but even so the situation was fairly dire and with war breaking out, urgent measures were needed.

As a matter of extreme urgency, more land had to be made available to grow crops. The Emergency Powers Act of 1939 gave the Minister of Agriculture authority – some said draconian powers – to direct and control food production, including the right to repossess any farm or terminate tenancies where the land was neglected or poorly cultivated. War Agricultural Committees, known to everyone as War Ags., were appointed for each county and immediately set about increasing home food production. From spring 1939 farm labourers wages increased and farmers were offered financial incentives to plough up grassland. Some farmers commented rather bitterly that the government only took an interest in farming when the nation was in danger – in December 1940, for instance, at a meeting of the National Farmers' Union (NFU) in Uckfield, that was reported in the *Sussex Express and County Herald,* the

Chairman voiced his opinion that 'for many years past farming has been the Cinderella of industries and shamefully neglected by each succeeding government' – but nevertheless farmers were offered £2 an acre for every acre they ploughed up between May and September 1939, which could then be used to grow wheat, oats, barley and potatoes. In what was known as the 'ploughing up' campaign, or the 'Battle for Wheat', the aim was to have an extra 2 million acres producing food by the harvest of 1940. Tractor drivers and other farming mechanics were exempted from conscription, farmers worked around the clock and by and large the target was reached. The process of reclamation continued after 1940: by the end of the war arable land had gone up by about 50 per cent from some 12 million acres to almost 18 million acres.

> Back to the Land, we must all lend a hand,
> To the farms and the fields we must go.
> There's a job to be done,
> Though we can't fire a gun
> We can still do our bit with the hoe.
> When your muscles are strong
> You will soon get along,
> And you'll think that a country life's grand.
> We're all needed now,
> We must all speed the plough,
> So come with us – Back to the Land.
>
> Back to the Land, with its clay and its sand,
> Its granite and gravel and grit,
> You grow barley and wheat
> And potatoes to eat
> To make sure the nation keeps fit.
> Remember the rest
> Are all doing their best,
> To achieve the results they have planned
> We will tell you once more
> You can help with the war
> If you come with us – Back to the Land
>
> (Official Land Army Song, *Back to the Land*. Words by P. Adkins and J. Moncrief. Music by E.K. Loring; all three were land girls)

One former Land Army member, Beryl Peacham, who served in the Land Army from 1943-49, and whose parents were tenant farmers on a 70-acre farm called Grandturzel, near Burwash, Sussex, remembered the War Ag arriving:

> …It was originally a dairy farm but when the War Ag got going on the farmers, they tried to tip us out; it was absolute murder, the way poor Mum had to stick up for me, she told me to go and do something else. There were three of them, a farmer from Sussex Downs, the Ministry man and another man. They wanted to take the farm so they could use it for whatever they wanted or to put anyone there. They managed to take so many farms and people never got them back, so I understand, that was the most terrible thing. Mum fought like a tom cat, she had the answer for everything and they put us on a sort of probation and a chap came from Fairlight to see us every couple of months.

Eventually, Beryl's family turned more than half the acreage over to wheat, barley and oats for the duration of the war, including one field that was 'absolutely peppered with anthills', but reclaiming grassland for arable was only one of the emergency measures. What farming needed was more workers – and it was this need that led to the re-emergence of the WLA.

Bringing in Women

Interestingly, and in stark contrast to the First World War, the Government realized early on that if war came, women would play a significant role: in the services, in the labour force and in support roles on the Home Front, a realization and recognition partly based on what women had achieved during the First World War but also in the knowledge that air attacks would bring war directly into people's homes in a way that had never happened before.

Life for women on the eve of the Second World War was very different from life in 1914. For a start, women now had a political voice: propertied women over the age of 30 had gained the vote in 1918; equal voting rights with men were gained in 1928 and by 1938 there were fifteen women MPs in the House of

Commons. Women had also made advances in all fields and, as the 1930s progressed, women of all classes were employed in greater numbers. In 1939, nearly 5 million women were in paid employment but most worked in low-paid, low-status areas, such as clothing and textiles. Increasing numbers were working as shop assistants or in offices as clerks and typists; only a handful were getting through to higher-status civil service jobs. Women were also making their way into the professions but still in quite small numbers. In 1928, for instance, there were only 21 women architects in Britain, 10 female chartered accountants, and only 82 women dentists. The main professions open to women were teaching and nursing; in 1938 some 134,000 women were working in the teaching profession and 154,000 women were employed in nursing. Cambridge University did not appoint its first woman professor until 1939.

The fact that the British government realized that women would be needed to fight the coming war was, in itself, a major change from 1914 but even so stereotypical images of 'a woman's place' were still all pervasive and influenced the thinking of many people so that opposition to women being employed in so-called 'men's work' continued to be widespread. Despite women's achievements during the First World War, farming was one of the areas still considered highly unsuitable for women. For some female veterans of the First World War, particularly for those who set out to re-create the WLA, the hurdles that had to be overcome were only too familiar.

As in the First World War, it was women of the upper and privileged classes who were called on to form the initial women's wartime organizations and who filled the upper echelons of these organizations. In May 1938, as part of the preparations for war, the Home Secretary Sir Samuel Hoare asked the Marchioness of Reading to form the Women's Voluntary Services for Air Raid Precautions; better known as the WVS, it was launched in June 1938, with the aim of training women to protect their homes and families in the event of air attack or invasion. Some 32,000 women enrolled, many recruited through privileged women's networks. The Auxiliary Territorial Service (ATS) was launched at much the same time.

Staffed almost entirely by women and headed by Dame Helen Gwynne Vaughan, its aim was to provide a supporting role for men in the army. And in June 1939, with war almost on the doorstep, the Ministry of Agriculture decided that the WLA should be reformed, with Lady Denman at its head.

Re-forming the Women's Land Army

Lady Gertrude ('Trudie') Denman was an efficient and energetic woman and the ideal person to be director of the WLA. Vita Sackville-West, historian of the Land Army and herself a Kent Land Army rep, described her as 'the most competent and experienced of chairmen'. From a privileged and wealthy family, she had a deep interest in, and knowledge of, country matters and, as Assistant Director of the Women's Branch of Food Production at the Ministry of Agriculture during the First World War, she had worked closely with Dame Meriel Talbot in recruiting for the original WLA. She had played a major role in the development of the Women's Institutes and in 1917 was elected chair of the National Federation of the Women's Institutes, a post that she held until her retirement in 1946. Lady Denman's organizational skills, experience and influential networks were second to none; she saw clearly the role that the WLA would play in the coming war, and had absolutely no doubt that their efforts would help to win the war. For her the war would be won 'in the fields of Britain' – little wonder then that she was the prime mover in getting the Land Army off the ground again.

Unfortunately the Ministry of Agriculture was not as perceptive, speedy or efficient as this remarkable woman and, as a result, Lady Denman's energetic work was constantly being blocked. The Ministry had actually approached Lady Denman in April 1938, following a top-level meeting to discuss the state of farm labour in the event of war. At that meeting it was decided that arrangements should be put in place for 'setting up a Women's branch of the Ministry in time of war' and that Lady Denman was the woman to carry out this work. It was clear that the Land Army would be run on a county basis, so Lady Denman was also asked to compile a list of women who could head county committees and advise on how they would function. However, it would take more than a year for the Land Army to come into being.

Initially Lady Denman was reluctant to take on the task: she was 54 and had only recently recovered from a serious illness; she was also heavily committed to her work with the Women's Institute and was worried that a Land Army role would detract from this, not least because she was working out what the Women's Institute's role should be in wartime. Shrewdly, however, Lady Denman realized that the two roles were complementary and that the Women's Institutes themselves would be a source of first-class womanpower: she could draw on key and trusted people from their ranks and the organization itself provided a county based network that would be invaluable. With support from the Federation, she decided to take up the challenge and immediately began drawing up detailed plans for a wartime Land Army. By May 1938, just one month after the meeting, she had chosen the women whom she felt would best fill the key posts and had written to them in strict confidence, telling them that in the event of war she would like them to form and head county committees to administer the Land Army.

The Ministry of Agriculture was much slower to commit. Lady Denman wrote to the Minister, Mr Dorman Smith, several times asking him to meet with her proposed county chairmen – Chair or Chairwoman were not terms used at that time – and discuss her proposals for setting up the WLA but it was not until March 1939 that she finally got a meeting with him. Once there, she put forward well thought out proposals and suggested that the county chairmen she had chosen should immediately be given permission to find out which farmers would take on land girls in their counties and where billets could be found. Her fear was that if her chosen administrators were not engaged at once in this way, she would lose them to the other women's wartime organizations. She also pressed the Minister to make a decision on minimum wages for land girls – the question of pay and benefits for land girls was one that would recur and ultimately lead to her resignation.

The response from officialdom was not just lukewarm, it was dismissive: the Treasury wrote to the Ministry describing Lady

Denman's ideas as 'a sledge hammer to crack a nut' and nothing happened. The Ministry's recalcitrance was infuriating. Lady Denman knew there was a real chance of losing her key officials if the Ministry did not make a commitment so in April she threatened to resign unless she was allowed to choose and appoint her headquarters staff immediately. Her threat worked: she was given the go ahead and on 1 June 1939 the WLA came into being once more. It was part of the Ministry of Agriculture but entirely staffed and run by women, the Ministry of Agriculture having given Lady Denman permission to prepare the Land Army in readiness for war, exactly on the lines that she had proposed.

Setting up Headquarters

Lady Denman promptly appointed a personal assistant, Mrs Inez Jenkins, a tried and trusted member of the Women's Institute and former General Secretary of the National Federation. Local Education Authorities and farmers were approached and asked to be ready to train women in tractor driving and other skilled farm work and a recruitment campaign for land girls began immediately. Not all farmers were at all happy about this and many were reluctant to use land girls. County committees were given official recognition, salaried secretaries and staff were appointed for each county committee and a conference of county chairmen, which Lady Denman had been asking for, finally took place in London. Commenting later, the Agriculture Ministry's Permanent Secretary said that in his long experience of conferences, he had 'never seen business despatched so quickly and speeches so relevant and short'.

Finally, on 29 August 1939, just five days before war broke out, the general headquarters of the new WLA were set up in Lady Denman's own magnificent country home, Balcombe Place in Sussex, which was transformed, re-arranged and turned over entirely to the needs of the WLA. More than 40 secretaries, clerks and other officers, mostly recruited from the Ministry of Agriculture, were sent down from London to staff, work and live in the new headquarters. The Ministry also insisted that one of their higher officials should be housed at Balcombe Place to deal with finances and to correspond with government departments and local authorities. In keeping with the social class of their director, when they arrived at Balcombe station they were met by a fleet of cars, including Lady Denman's Rolls Royce, to transport them to Balcombe Place where they were given cocktails while they waited for their bedrooms to be allocated.

The whole of Balcombe Place was turned into a smoothly running business-like operation. Oak panelling and rich draperies provided a backcloth to a hive of industry, as bedrooms were turned into offices, stables and outhouses were turned into warehouses for numerous Land Army uniforms and, in 1940, a monthly magazine, the *Land Girl*, was started under the editorship of Mrs Margaret Pyke who, like Lady Denman, was a pioneering birth control campaigner. Under her competent editorship, the *Land Girl* was produced throughout the war and reached a circulation of more than 21,000 copies.

By all accounts, life at headquarters was extremely pleasant – Lady Denman made sure that everyone was extremely well looked after and cared for – rationing was stringent but even so meals were excellent, there were swimming and tennis facilities, electric kettles for tea-making, a laundry room for washing and plenty of opportunities for recreation. Conditions were more luxurious than those enjoyed by the thousands of land girls who would soon be working up and down the country but Balcombe Place rapidly became a hive of industry, as Vita Sackville-West described in her book *The Women's Land Army*:

A representative came round every month, one of the organisers. She lived in Northiam. She was a bit posh.

(Helen Dawson, 84, former land girl, Sussex)

...the splendid rooms are now filled with office-desks and trestle tables, piled with card-indexes and stationery, typewriters and telephones, pots of paste and Stickphast. Green and white posters of Land-girls leading horses, Land-girls carrying corn-sheaves, are tacked up with drawing pins against the walls. Busy young women carrying folders run nimbly up and down the wide oak staircase; the doors of the rooms on the upper floor, which once were spare bedrooms, are now labelled with the designation of the office-department to be found within. In one window embrasure sits the editorial staff of The Land-girl monthly magazine…Nor is this hive of activity restricted to the house itself. Out of doors, in the garden and on the now sacrificed lawn-tennis courts, is a variety of live-stock…One of the queerest sights in the trans-formation of Balcombe is the occupation by Land Army uniform of the outbuildings – the garages, the stables, and the squash-rackets court. These evidences of luxury have become purely utilitarian; they have been turned into ware-houses…

It was quite a venture – and it needed to be because the WLA was a big organization. Administratively, England and Wales were divided into seven regions, each consisting of one or more counties. Seven regional officers were based at the headquarters in Balcombe Place, where they acted as liaison officers between headquarters and the counties. Each county had its own office, or in the case of larger counties, more than one office, so that in all there were 52 county offices. Each had its own county officers – organizing secretary, committee, sub-committee and local rep-resentatives. Every county committee had a county chairman and secretary – in fact the *Land Girl Manual*, a rather jolly and very patriotic publication written by W.E. Shewell-Cooper and published in 1941, listed each of the county chairmen at the back of the book, together with their addresses and telephone numbers, so they could be accessed directly by all members. County secretaries, officers and clerical staff were on salaries but the chairwomen, local representatives and committee members worked on a voluntary basis and were all unpaid. The day-to-day grassroots organizing of the Land Army took place at county level but county officers had to report to regional offices, which in turn reported back to the Balcombe Place head-quarters. For Vita Sackville-West, the Balcombe Place headquarters was the 'big, pumping heart at the centre of the organization', while the county offices were 'the ends of the arteries'.

Complex Administration

The administration was massive and also quite complex: over the course of the war, which finally broke out on 3 September 1939, more than 80,000 women enlisted in the Land Army and each one of them needed meticulous records, from initial application forms and medical records, through to details of where they worked, who they worked for, what work they were doing, plus information about their pay and billeting arrangements. Local representatives, county offices and staff at headquarters had myriad tasks: they were not only dealing with constant queries from land girls about pay, medical and other welfare matters, clothing and billets but also had to liaise with various government officials, labour exchanges, the Agricultural Wage Boards and trade unions, notably the National Union of Farmers, the Transport and General Workers Union and the National Union of Agricultural Workers. Land Army officers dealt with recruitment, requisitioning, checking of billets, running hostels, farmers, equipment and welfare matters. To some extent the complexity of the administration reflected the fact that the Land Army itself was a special case: unlike women in the armed forces, land girls were not employed by the state, nor subject to military rules and discipline; they were employed by individual farmers, who received payment from the state but nevertheless could dismiss land girls. Land girls themselves, by definition, were often isolated so that the task of maintaining contact with the workforce was itself difficult. It says a great deal for the efficiency and caring attitudes of Land Army administrators, from Lady Denman down to county level, as well as the dedication of the land girls themselves, that the dropout rate from the Land Army was very low compared with women in other wartime services.

Lady Denman made good use of her contacts in the Women's Institute, calling on many of them to help her run the WLA. There were criticisms that county and regional chairwomen were rather upper-crust and therefore somewhat far removed from the social status of most of the land girls themselves but, for Lady Denman, these women were experienced in country-side matters; they had first-hand knowledge of problems associated with employing agricultural workers and also were acquainted with the farmers in their areas, something that was very useful in the early stages when many farmers were extremely reluctant to make use of the land girls. They had the contacts and the local knowledge.

Semi-independent Status

From day one, Lady Denman was a hands-on director. Throughout the war years, she travelled constantly around the country, visiting every county and regional officer and maintaining personal contact not just with administrators but also with members of the Land Army themselves. She worked tirelessly to promote the Land Army and to improve the status and conditions of the land girls under her direction, something that led her into many tensions and confrontations with government ministers. Initially the WLA came under the direct control of the Ministry of Agriculture and there were difficulties as Lady Denman fought one battle after another with the Ministry for support – their approach to early recruitment for instance was often lacklustre and they did not do as much as they could to encourage farmers to take up land girls. In the spring of 1941 Lady Denman managed to wrest control from the Ministry and the WLA was given semi-independent status with Lady Denman personally responsible for the entire running of it.

At this point, Lady Denman approached Buckingham Palace and asked if the Queen would consider becoming the WLA patron. The Queen accepted and throughout the war, and afterwards, took an active interest in the Land Army's activities. She reviewed land girls, subscribed to the WLA Benevolent Fund, which was set up later in the war and, in 1943, when the Land Army reached its fourth birthday, threw a birthday party at Buckingham Palace for more than 300 land girls. The royal family themselves also employed land girls on their estates.

Lady Gertrude Denman (1884-1954)

The late Nineteenth and early Twentieth Centuries produced a number of remarkable and strong-minded women, who challenged the restrictions of the day to support and open up opportunities for women. Lady Denman was one of these. Throughout her life she worked untiringly for a number of extremely important women's organizations, among them the Women's Institute, the Family Planning Association and of course, the WLA.

She was born Gertrude Mary Pearson into great wealth, the second child and only daughter of Weeman Pearson, later Viscount Cowdray, an oil magnate and newspaper owner, and Annie Cass, a feminist and skilled organizer with many charitable interests. In 1903 she married Thomas Denman, third Baron Denman: the couple had two children but the marriage was not a success and after 1914 they lived fairly separate lives.

By all accounts Lady Denman was a remarkable women – courageous, determined, hard working, a brilliant organizer and utterly loyal to those she worked with and for. She also had an excellent sense of humour and fun. She never took her privilege or wealth for granted, but believed that with wealth came a responsibility to the community – and in her case, her commitment was first and foremost to women. She first demonstrated this when she was still a young woman, working for women's suffrage through the Executive of the Women's Liberal Federation. Never a militant suffragette, she believed in achieving change through peaceful, law-abiding means.

Later, after a three years' stint in Australia when her husband was appointed Governor General, she became involved in the growing Women's Institute movement, becoming the national Chairman in 1917. Today the WI has a rather dated image but that is to dismiss its early radicalism: under Trudie Denman's leadership, it became a formidable and highly democratic organization that gave countrywomen a voice and helped them to widen their horizons. Lady Denman was acutely aware of the particular nature of rural poverty and deprivation, and through the WI worked to open up rural education and opportunities.

In 1930 Lady Denman widened her public work when she became first chairman of the Family Planning Association: once more her interest in this field was based on her concern for women, in particular the damaging impact on women, particularly poor women, of constant child bearing; like the Women's Co-operative Movement, she believed that women should be able to control their own fertility to produce children when they wanted. Through this work, which she continued throughout her life, she became close friends with Margaret Pyke, another birth control pioneer, who later worked with Gertrude Denman in the WLA, helping to produce the Land Army magazine.

Lady Denman was particularly interested in rural affairs: she experimented with poultry breeding at Balcombe Place and, during the First World War, worked with the Ministry of Food and the WLA. A brilliant organizer and chairman, she was therefore the obvious person to approach to re-form the Land Army in the Second World War. She served as Honorary Director of the Land Army from 1939, giving her time, energies and absolute commitment to the organization – making her home available for its headquarters and maintaining a constant hands-on approach. She was absolutely committed to the well being of the thousands of young women who enlisted in the Land Army: she fought constantly for the Land Army to receive better conditions and for the recognition it deserved and in 1945 finally resigned in protest against the refusal of the government to provide post-war benefits for the land girls.

Lady Denman died in 1954. Hundreds of letters of sympathy flooded in from women whose lives had been touched by her work. Queen Elizabeth, the Queen Mother referred to Lady Denman's 'courage and integrity in public life and the selfless service which she gave with such wisdom and humanity especially to the cause of women' and at the memorial service at Balcombe Parish Church held a week after her death, the Bishop of Chichester paid tribute to her 'determination to do everything she could to help the women of her country...'.

* * *

Chapter 3

Recruitment and Propaganda

*F*or *a healthy, happy job join The Women's Land Army*

(Recruiting slogan)

NO SOONER had the Women's Land Army been set up, than it began recruiting for members. From June 1939 recruitment offices or depots were set up in each county, recruitment posters were produced and notices appeared in newspapers appealing for women to join the WLA: war had not yet broken out so the initial aim was to set up a work force in waiting that was trained and ready to go anywhere if, and as soon as, war began.

Appealing for Women

Letters from county chairwomen appeared in newspapers up and down the country: this appeal, which appeared in the *Sussex Express and County Herald* of 16 June 1939 from Diana Countess de la Warr, chair of the East Sussex Committee of the WLA, was typical. In it she asked the newspaper to:

> ... bring to the notice of Sussex women and girls a branch of National Service which has, up till now, received very little publicity, the Women's Land Army.
>
> The need not only for maintaining, but for increasing our home-grown food supply in wartime is obvious. Now, with the introduction of military service for men between the ages of 20 and 21, which will, it is estimated, affect 25,000 agricultural workers each year, the need for women land workers will be more urgent than ever.

When one recognises that every ton of extra food grown in this country will mean a ton less to be carried here from overseas, with all the risks which that entails to our merchantmen and convoy ships and when one remembers how near this country came to defeat in the last war, through the submarine menace to our food supplies, then it is easy to realise that in a future war, food production will be a work of vital importance – a work in which women will have to play an active part.

At least 50,000 women will be needed. Although they would only be called upon in the event of war, we want them to enrol in the Women's Land Army now, either as full-time workers in their own districts, or as members of a mobile force ready to work in any part of the country, or indeed as part-time workers, if their home duties will not allow them to devote all their time to agriculture.

The Government has now appointed women's committees in every county to assist with the organization of the Land Army. One of the first activities of these committees will be to arrange short courses of training in farm work and tractor driving for those volunteers who are able to take them.

In the meantime we ask every woman who is prepared to volunteer for work on the land in time of war to register her name by filling up the form in the National Service Guide, obtainable at any Post Office or enrolling themselves at the local branch of Women's Voluntary Services.

As chairman of the East Sussex Committee of the Women's Land Army, I urge all Sussex women who have not already joined some branch of National Service to give this appeal their earnest consideration.

Any woman wishing to enrol in the Land Army was expected to present herself at a recruitment office where she had to satisfy the local WLA committee that she had the physical stamina and aptitude for farming work, as well as the commitment to stick to the work. If she was accepted, the recruit was enrolled and told to hold herself in readiness to report for duty as and when she was called to do so. Provided she had no family commitments, the recruits in the early stages anyway, were told that they might be sent anywhere in the country and would be expected to do whatever farming work was required. At this point, recruits then returned to their peacetime occupations until further notice.

One early recruit was Peggy Pearce, 90, who joined the Land Army at the outbreak of war when she was about 22. She was living in Forest Hill, working in the hat department of a major store when she decided to volunteer:

> ...I met a friend, a girl there, she lived in Forest Hill and we palled up, and I happened to say 'I want to go in the Land Army', because as a child, my mother came from a big farming family in Bury St Edmunds, every summer my brother and I...went to grandma and grandpa's farm for about four weeks. My friend and I wanted to go on the land. An office was opened in London; I've forgotten where. First of all we went up and they said 'Well, you're about the first people', so it was some time before we actually got called up, well it was a new thing, and then the Land Girls had to go to the agricultural college for a month, outside Gloucester. It was the most beautiful mansion, and when we got there, there were masses of these girls all walking about, looking suspiciously at each other, thinking 'oh gosh, she must know what's going to happen', but it turned out we were all new... Each week you had to do something different, it was either poultry, or you had your arms up cheese making – I couldn't bear that – and on the land...I chose to stay with my friend and went into mixed farming. You got the cows up at 6 in the morning, hand milked them, and then had to clean out and then we went in for breakfast, so we were glad we went in for that because you were out in a field, perhaps 10-acre field, on your own, hoeing blooming cabbages and it was quite nice to think, perhaps I can go in and get the cows. And when you'd done the four weeks, they'd find a farm for you to go to...

Land Army recruitment was directed at women who were not already working in agriculture so farmers' wives and other existing farm workers were excluded. Veteran land girls from the First World War however, if physically fit, were warmly invited to rejoin.

Typists Drive Tractors

A Land Girl's Memories

A Land Girl I chose to be
To save my king and country.
Out in the wind, the rain, and the sun
You see there was a war to be won.

So off to college to learn my trade
I was chosen to be a dairymaid.
To milk the cows at 4 o'clock
And keep an eye on all the stock.
I'd make the butter all creamy and
    gold
Patterned and packed, ready to be
    sold.

A Land Girl I was meant to be,
I guess it was my destiny.
I enjoyed those days though the work
    was hard
But we won the war that was my
    reward.

Mrs Helen Dawson (née Buss), 2007.
Helen Dawson served in the Women's Land Army from 1945-48, working on farms in Bodiam, Sussex.

As inexperienced recruits came forward, the Land Army arranged training for them. Short but intensive training courses were set up designed specifically for Land Army recruits at agricultural colleges such as Wye and Plumpton or on specially selected farms, and very soon early recruits were going through the process. In July 1939 the *Sussex Express and County Herald* ran a feature, entitled 'Typists Drive Tractors at Plumpton', which described some of the first intake of Land Army recruits who were attending two weeks' training at Wales Farm, Plumpton, organized by the county council in co-operation with the East Sussex School of Agriculture.

Presenting the training as a 'new way for girls to spend a holiday', a common approach before war broke out, the feature described how the young recruits spent twelve hours a day, with breaks for meals, learning to drive and manage tractors and how to plough. According to the reporter, the 'typists, library assistants and housewives', one of whom was apparently a 'rosy-cheeked brunette', were extremely keen and happily coming to terms with managing the tractors, something that none of them had ever done before, and which the reporter described as 'heavy things for girls to handle'. The article went on to paint a rosy picture of enthusiastic young girls discarding dance frocks and fashionable hats in favour of knee breeches and rubber waders to spend their time learning how to plough a straight furrow with a cumbersome tractor that required strenuous cranking to start it up and considerable strength to steer while simultaneously operating the mower. The instructor, a Mr Beard, was quoted as saying that the young women were 'doing splendidly…[and]…learning quicker than a good many men students I have met.' Sadly, however, not everyone was as positive as Mr Beard about the WLA when it was first formed.

A Working Holiday
Land Army work is something which girls and women of all types and ages will find interesting and health-giving, and the only qualification is a reasonable standard of fitness. The period of training is only a fortnight, and those who would find a country holiday attractive and are prepared to pay £1 for their board should find the training period as enjoyable as it is instructive.
(*Hastings Observer*, 22 July 1939)

Eager Recruits and Reluctant Farmers

Despite women's achievements during the First World War, old prejudices died hard and there was considerable opposition from trade unionists, male workers, servicemen, and husbands to employing women in areas of work normally done by men. The issue of employing married women, with or without children, was particularly contentious – a marriage bar still operated in various jobs which meant that on marriage, women had to leave certain professions – and there was much talk in the newspapers about the employment of women destroying or damaging home life, particularly if women were sent away from home. Lurid images were conjured up of a tired and weary husband returning home to an empty house, with no meal on the table.

Attitudes such as these affected women's involvement in many areas of war work – women who worked as engineers and welders in the armaments industries, for instance, encountered considerable discrimination from male workers and trade unions – but those who wanted to help the war effort by working in agriculture faced particular prejudice and discouragement.

By the time war was declared on 3 September 1939, some 17,000 women had volunteered for the WLA and about 1,000 were ready to be put straight to work, most of them having received training. The new recruits, mostly in their late teens or early twenties, were eager to get to work. Vita Sackville-West told of a young recruit who had put her name down, and when she was called and asked how long she needed to get ready, had replied, 'Can you give me twenty minutes?' On 29 September 1939 Countess de La Warr sent another letter to the *Sussex Express and County Herald*, this time letting farmers know that land girls were ready and available for work:

...I should be very grateful if you would bring to the attention of farmers in East Sussex the fact that the Women's Land Army is now in a position to supply trained and partially trained women ready to go out on to farms as milkers, tractor drivers, and general farm workers. These Land Army workers fall into two categories...(a) those who are fully trained...and experienced in one of the branches of agriculture and (b) those who have taken a four week course at...Plumpton or on a specially selected training farm and have therefore some experience [of] farming work. We have also a large number of untrained girls who are anxious to go on to farms as trainees. The Government is willing to pay farmers 15/- a week as a board and lodging allowance...All inquiries from farmers wishing to employ Land Army workers should be made to the East Sussex Organising Secretary... .

Many farmers, however, were not nearly as enthusiastic as the new recruits and some were extremely reluctant to have young women foisted onto them, particularly those who came from towns and cities. They wanted men to work on the land and, in response to their demands, call up of male agricultural labourers was temporarily halted.

There were various objections to using women. There was a deeply entrenched prejudice against women working on the land. Despite everything that the WLA had achieved just twenty years earlier, many farmers felt that agriculture was a man's world in which there was no place for women, particularly inexperienced women from towns and cities. One farmer writing in the *Sussex Express and County Herald* commented that most townspeople had 'not the slightest idea what is expected' and assumed that at least 50 per cent of them 'would crack up under the strain'. In his opinion, tractor driving was 'a lad's job'; the idea that a woman should be in the driving seat was quite unthinkable.

Farming unions were also worried that women land workers would undercut the already low wages of male agricultural workers and indeed, initially, the basic rate of pay for a land girl was 28/- a week, ten shillings below the basic wage of a male agricultural worker. Some of their opposition was fuelled by long-standing grievances against successive Governments, which had failed, in the view of the farming community, to assist a depressed industry. In June 1939, the National Union of Agricultural Workers announced its decision to boycott the WLA because there was no assurance that the interests of the highly skilled – and male – workers on the land would be safeguarded. Instead the Union argued that although they supported the principle of using women workers, the Government had not consulted with them about wages and conditions and unless the position was clarified, the 'farming community will be obliged to regard the W.L.A. as another instance of the frivolous attitude of the National Government to food production in this country, and another manifestation of the pernicious assumption that anybody can farm'. Some farmers complained that short training courses could not possibly equip women with the necessary skills to carry out farming duties and some even said that their wives would not like them to employ land girls.

They [farmers] didn't think a girl could do a man's job I expect, but they got shook up.

(Hazel King, tractor driver, Romney Marsh, Kent)

Agricultural journals and union magazines made no secret of their opposition to the use of women and their view that using women to do men's work was absurd. At times prejudice was presented in a highly facetious fashion, designed to raise a chuckle in the male-dominated world of farming. An editorial in the *Land Worker*, the magazine of the National Union of Agricultural Workers, even managed to bring the Bible into the argument claiming – not for the first time – that it was a woman's fault that Adam fell from grace, and that the Garden of Eden 'was a successful holding utterly wrecked by the employment of women in the fruit-picking season', a witty, if heavy handed observation that doubtless raised a chuckle but certainly demonstrated the almost endemic sexism within farming unions at that time.

The Government did little to counteract the flow of bad publicity, much to the annoyance of Lady Denman and her colleagues. In 1940, Ernest Bevin, then Minister of Labour, took over responsibility for women's mobilization but although the Ministry of Agriculture was urging the WLA to recruit more members, Government broadcasts aimed at farmers who needed more labour, including a broadcast made by Bevin, encouraged them to apply to their local labour exchanges or to the War Ag – there were no suggestions that farmers should approach the WLA, something that WLA administrators commented on, and criticized, in letters to newspapers and Government officials.

The tendency to ignore the WLA was reflected in an appeal that Lord Beaverbrook published in the *Daily Express* in 1940 under the heading 'We Have Yet to Sow the Seeds of Victory'. In this Beaverbrook exhorted the British population to make greater efforts to increase food production, putting forward detailed plans that ranged from putting more acreage under cultivation, increasing the milk yield, cultivating allotments and turning gardens over to vegetables. They were all good suggestions and were part of the overall push to raise consciousness about the need for home-produced food supplies. Tellingly Beaverbrook called for 'every available man...to be turned to agricultural pursuits' and suggested that 'Labourers must be called back not only from the Army, but also from city occupations. Wherever an experienced farm hand can be found he should be persuaded to return at once to the cultivation of the soil...' There were references to the need to use women but no acknowledgement of the enormous efforts that the WLA was already making. Instead, Beaverbrook stated that 'The Government should also provide means for training women...' and went on to claim that '...they [women] would be especially suitable to look after pigs and poultry. And the male labour which they would replace, can be directed quite easily to other agricultural pursuits...'

Attitudes such as these, and the fact that the Ministry of Agriculture was itself pressing the Cabinet to postpone military service for agricultural workers, meant that although young women were flocking to the WLA, it was extremely difficult to place them in work and many of the new recruits either had to be sent home, back to queues at the labour exchanges or, if they were lucky, back to their civilian occupations, and told to wait until they were called on. Not all farmers, however, were opposed to the WLA and some were highly frustrated by the situation. In January 1940 an article in the *Picture Post* referred to a letter from a Hampshire farmer which appeared in the correspondence columns of *The Times* in which he said 'The disappointment in official quarters is negligible to that felt alike by farmers at the Government's lack of action in not bringing milk prices into line with cost, and by land girls whose killed enthusiasm and wasted training is a sacrifice on the altar of political expediency and incompetence'.

Not surprisingly, when a second major recruitment drive happened in 1940, the take up was slow as some women turned to find war work in other areas. Infuriated by this and by the fact that the two Government radio broadcasts had failed to mention the WLA, Lady Denman wrote to the Rt. Hon. Robert Hudson, who had recently been appointed Minister of Agriculture complaining about the situation and saying that she was:

> ...most distressed to hear Mr Hurd in his broadcast last night advise farmers wanting seasonal labour to apply either to the War Ag Cttee or Labour Exchange. This will give farmers the impression that the Ministry does not consider the Land Army seriously as a source of labour and it must

add to the already loudly expressed dissatisfaction of the many volunteers whom the Land Army enrolled for seasonal work and who are now being told that they are not likely to be needed. Mr Hurd's omission is particularly unfortunate as...I am receiving protests that when discussing agricultural labour he [Ernest Bevin, Minister for Labour] did not mention the Land Army. These broadcasts will add to our troubles...For the regular force we have recruited about 3,000 of the additional 5,000 volunteers we were told to enrol. Many...are already in training, but as yet we have not got enough jobs for them...Now, even the small demands which we have received for...workers are being cancelled, partly because soldiers are being made available for farm labour at a very low rate...

Lady Denman finished by asking Hudson to make a special reference to the WLA in a radio broadcast that he was due to make the following day. Hudson did so, which won him the thanks of Lady Denman, who told him it was a pleasure 'to hear the Land Army mentioned individually and not as one item of a mixed bag of conchies, prisoners of war, unemployed etc.!'. He went on to become one of the WLA's staunchest supporters and allies, promoting and championing their work and their value.

Dame Meriel Talbot also joined the fray and wrote a letter to *The Times* in which she called for a 'truce to criticism', saying:

... In a recent issue of *The Times* it was reported that Mr Hudson, Minister of Agriculture, when speaking at a meeting of farmers and others, deplored the present spate of criticism of the Women's Land Army as 'the height of folly and short-sightedness'. Can it be that the experience, hardly won, of the last War has been forgotten?

I write as one who served as Director of the first Women's Land Army. At that time both criticism and scepticism were to be expected for farmers, except in a few areas, had never employed women as whole-time wage earners and were naturally sceptical of their ability either to do skilled work or to stick to it. Yet by the end of the War, criticism had vanished. The girls, carefully selected, tested, and enrolled in the new mobile Land Army, had proved their willingness and ability to do skilled work of varying kinds on farms large and small...

... If this was so 22 years ago, can we doubt that with the extension of physical fitness, the development of motor-driving, and every kind of outdoor sport, members of the present Women's Land Army are capable of surpassing the pioneers? I would urge the critics and sceptics to make themselves aware of the facts, and to help and not hinder the production of home-grown food, and the call for man-power elsewhere at this grave time...

Turning the Tide of Prejudice

Ultimately, however, and as in the previous war, it was the hard work and determination of the land girls themselves that did more to open farmers' closed minds than anything else. Growing demands on farmers as the war progressed and increasing shortage of male workers as men were conscripted to fight, also helped to overcome early prejudice. By December 1939, despite all the difficulties, some 4,500 land girls had been placed in work. The winter of 1939/40 was harsh and bitter – one of the worst in living memory – but despite the dreadful conditions, the newly recruited and trained land girls, many of whom came from towns and had had no previous experience of farming, played a full part in ploughing up the required extra 2 million acres of land, ready for sowing in spring 1940. By June 1940 some 6,000 land girls were being employed and letters and recommendations from farmers began to appear in local newspapers as the word spread that land girls, despite all the anxieties, were proving themselves to be an invaluable work force.

As the *Picture Post* observed: 'The farmers who have employed girls and the agricultural teachers who have trained them say they are delighted with the girls' progress. Failures actually on the farm have been negligible.' Commenting on the furore around employing land girls, the *Picture Post* went on to say that 'Everybody has had their say about the Women's Land Army except the women themselves. Right or wrong, they've been getting on with their training and, skilled or unskilled...are already doing their bit on the farm.'

Although arguments about the use of land girls continued to rumble on, negative attitudes began to shift. In March 1940, an editorial in the *Sussex Express* stated that it was obvious that 'fuller use will have to be made of the Women's Land Army' and referred to the fact that 'The women who are employed at present are winning golden opinions for their zeal and capabilities.'

As war got underway in earnest, what was also becoming increasingly clear was that the role of the WLA was going to be an essential and critical element in winning the war. Robert Hudson, Minister of Agriculture, emphasized the point in October 1940 in a message that he addressed to members of the WLA and which was published in the *Land Girl*:

Total war is a war of endurance and to ensure winning it we must make the utmost use of all our resources, especially the land. Milking the cows, feeding the pigs and poultry or driving a tractor day after day, is unspectacular and at times may seem to you very dull. But without the food you help to produce, the bravery of the fighting services would be of no avail and the machinery in our munitions factories would be silent and still. Famine could achieve what no bomb or blitzkrieg or invading force will ever bring about. It is your vital task to see that such a thing could in no conceivable circumstances arise, and is driven even further from the realms of possibilities. (*Land Girl* magazine, October 1940)

Compulsory Call-Up

Prejudice against women working in what were considered to be men's jobs and the slow mobilization of women were not confined to the WLA. Although it was clear that women were needed in what was to become a 'total war', it took time to mobilize them. When war broke out, many women were actually thrown out of work. Women's unemployment rose sharply because most women were employed in areas such as clothing and textiles, which were geared to the consumer market. This left a pool of labour available for the war effort but, initially, the Government did not intervene to shift unemployed women into war work. They took a fairly laissez-faire attitude and left well alone. As a result, many women went into the war years on the dole.

Women's response to war in 1939 was also slightly different from that in 1914. At the outbreak of war in 1914 jingoism and patriotism motivated large numbers of women, particularly those of the upper and middle-classes to offer their services immediately. In 1939, the response was slower, possibly because memories of the carnage of the First World War were only too recent.

By early 1941 the number of women in essential war work, such as munitions, farming and Government departments, was far lower than needed, even though more than 250,000 women were still unemployed. As a result, the Ministry of Labour under Ernest Bevin, took a more directive approach. From May 1941, all British women aged between 19 and 40 had to register at labour exchanges so the Ministry of Labour could see where women were and direct them into areas where they were needed. Theoretically women could choose whether to go into the services, industry, or the Land Army but, in essence, the Government had introduced compulsory call-up or conscription for women – the only one of the warring countries to do so. At much the same time, and in an attempt overcome male employers' entrenched attitudes towards women working in traditionally male arenas, the Government also issued the Essential Work Order (EWO), which compelled employers to take and keep women workers into the areas where they were directed. Later all women aged 19-51 were conscripted. The measures worked and by October 1943, nine out of ten single women and eight out of ten married women were working in the forces, the Land Army or in wartime industries. The total number of British women in war work was about 7,750,000 – 2 million more than in 1939.

The Government had also taken advice about how best to mobilize women, particularly from the Women's Consultative Committee, which included two women MPs, Edith

Summerskill and Irene Ward, women trade unionists and members of women's voluntary organizations. On the Committee's suggestion, it was decided that single women, without dependents, could and should be seen as a mobile work force and could be directed wherever they might be needed, while married women or those with dependants should be considered a non-mobile work force and could not be directed into work that would mean they had to leave home, but they could be put to work locally. To the great disappointment and annoyance of the Committee, the Government was not prepared to incorporate the principle of equal pay into wartime women's employment policies – that development would have to wait until the 1970s – but within a fairly short space of time, all women of employment age had been registered and by 1944 virtually all women of employable age were engaged in the war effort. It was later said that one of the reasons that Britain won the war was because the country made such good use of its women. Where they could, many women chose to volunteer for their chosen war work rather than wait to be compulsorily called up and directed against their wishes.

Growing Demand for Land Girls

As far as the Land Army went, appeals for more women to work on the land continued apace. At first the numbers grew slowly; by June 1941, two years after the WLA had been formed, there were still only 14,000 land girls, far fewer than in the First World War, but from then on demand and numbers increased rapidly as more men were called up to fight and attacks on shipping intensified, threatening food supplies. By June 1942, about 40,000 land girls were working on the land and a year later the figure had risen to 65,000. By the end of 1943, the total reached well over 80,000 or more and the War Cabinet decided that recruiting had to stop so that women could be channelled into other work, particularly munitions. Recruitment was later reintroduced when the Government realized that the Land Army would be needed after the war ended.

Recruitment Strategies

Recruitment into the Land Army operated in liaison with the Ministry of Labour. Women who wanted to join up either went to their local labour exchange, or to local recruiting depots. Some young women in rural areas were recruited directly by local farmers who already knew them. Would-be land girls were interviewed, given a medical and, if necessary, sent for training. Land Army recruiting offices were set up in most towns, although they were sometimes quite basic. A notice in the *Hastings Observer* on 16 September 1939, for instance, advised volunteers who wanted to join the WLA that they could enrol at a depot that had been established on the second floor of Messrs Plummer, Roddis, a store in Robertson Street, Hastings, where enrolments could take place between 11 a.m. – 1 p.m. each week day morning and between 4 p.m. – 6 p.m. every afternoon.

The WLA also held recruitment rallies at which land girls, dressed in their uniforms, paraded through the streets, or drove tractors encouraging other young women to come and join them. Women were encouraged to join the Land Army not only to release agricultural labourers for the armed forces but also becuase of the health and other physical benefits that women would gain from working on the land. Recruitment propaganda stressed the popularity of the Land Army and emphasized that joining the WLA was ideal for those women and girls who liked an open-air life. Well-designed posters were used for recruit-ment purposes, most of which presented a very romantic picture of healthy, smiling young women, cuddling lambs or standing beaming next to large cart horses, or in the middle of corn fields; they were effective propaganda but rarely realistic. They gave no impression at all of the hard, physical and taxing work that new recruits would find themselves doing nor, according to Eileen Hodd, 80, who joined the Land Army when she was just coming up to age 17, were the details correct: 'Well, for one thing, you didn't wear that shirt with those breeches, with that shirt you had summer overalls, not corduroy breeches, you had bib and braces...it wasn't quite like that...she's not dressed right for a start'. Funnily enough one recruitment poster that was widely used did feature an actual land girl but it had been printed without her knowledge. During her training, she was photographed with a newborn calf. She was unable to find the negative and later, to her great surprise, saw her image looking out at her from a recruitment poster.

As war continued, land girls were filmed driving tractors, ploughing up land and hoeing fields, and the films were also used for recruitment purposes.

Age and Health Checks

Strictly speaking women wanting to join the Land Army had to be aged between 18 and 40 but, in practice, some would-be land girls lied about their age and, as demand for workers increased, they got away with it. One was Sheelah Cruttenden, deceased, who lived near Bristol. She later wrote an account of her experiences:

> ...as a naïve sixteen-year-old I joined the Women's Land Army. The fact that I was underage was not found out until a pay rise was due the following year. Women enrolling came from all areas and all walks of life. Many came from the city like me who had been up until then working as a waitress at Carwardines Restaurant near Bristol. There I had occasionally served stage actors from the city theatres, such as Wendy Hillier. I was initially stationed for six months at a hostel in Shurdington, Gloucester. I was fortunate enough to have met two WLA girls on the station platform the day I arrived. These girls became good friends throughout my Land Army days and beyond...

Despite initially having been economic with the truth, Sheelah went on to serve continuously with the WLA until 1946, when she took a year's break, moved to Sussex and then re-joined in 1947 for a further two years. She finally left in 1949, her days in the Land Army having been 'some of the happiest in my life'.

Another under age recruit was Eileen Grabham, 81, a Londoner from Shoreditch, who joined the Land Army in 1943:

> I joined when I was 17 in '43. I was sent to Rye Marsh four miles from here [Brenzett, Kent] and we used to go to work

by bus, pick up girls from here then we used to go to a farm at Brooklands and I stayed there three months. I was doing general fieldwork, we helped with the harvest and we helped with peas. My very first job was, we called it 'thistle dodging', we all had a little hoe and we had to go round the field hoeing the thistles up; nowadays, they would use a spray. They sent me to Herne Bay but the hostel was in Smeltings, just outside and I was there for two months and then I was sent to a farm near Folkestone...I eventually married the farmer's son, not till after the war...

Recruits were given preliminary interviews, either in the recruiting office or sometimes, particularly in the case of young countrywomen, a WLA representative might interview them in their own home. Questions were fairly basic: did the recruit have any previous experience of farm work? Did she have any work preference? What size uniform did she need? What was her present occupation? Could she drive a car or bicycle? And did she have any experience of country life? Two references were also required.

All recruits were supposed to be given a medical but in many cases, according to former land girls, this could often be quite cursory. Joan Markby, 85, was 21 when she joined the Land Army in 1943. She was living in Bournemouth and working in Boscombe as a secretary:

I thought it would be lovely to be either a WRN or in the Land Army and then we did this sort of tossing up thing at the office to see whether I'd try to get into the WRNS or the Land Army...and it came down Land Army so they said, 'Do you want to be in Hampshire or Dorset?' I said Dorset because I liked the countryside and the openness down there so that's how it all happened. They checked our hearts and looked to see if we had flat feet, that's all, and we didn't have a tetanus injection...now I think how awful, but we didn't...nothing, no that was all there was and off we went for a month's training...

Another former Land Army member, Stella Hope:

…went along to the Labour Exchange and asked how I could join. Very shortly afterwards I received a notice to have a medical examination. Now that was a laugh. I walked into the office therefore I was fit. I think I answered a few questions but nothing of any significance that I can recall…

And, as with their ages, some women were so eager to join that they simply did not tell the truth. One was Mrs J.L. Stevens. She had been working as an invoice typist and wanted to join the Land Army in 1943 when she was 17. Her father objected so she waited until the following year when she was 18, and then applied. She was interviewed in Chelmsford but was so keen to join that she deliberately did not mention that she had suffered rheumatic fever when she was a child; her family doctor, too, did not disclose the information and she was accepted. Helen Dawson, 84, from Sussex was another former land girl who avoided disclosure. Describing herself as a 'shy country girl,' she joined the Land Army towards the end of the war, and said 'Actually I had a hernia but they didn't ask. I lied because I so wanted to get in.'

Chapter 4

Who Were the Land Girls?

Workers from shops and offices, mannequins, actresses, domestic servants and typists.

(Journal of the Ministry of Agriculture)

SO: WHO were the 'land girls' as members of the Women's Land Army were known? Who were the more than 80,000 women who worked on the land during the war, doing every task imaginable from harvesting and threshing through to milking, thistle docking and rat catching? Where did they come from? And why did they join?

Milliners and Manicurists

Land girls came from every conceivable walk of life and from all over Britain, with about one-third being recruited from London or the northern industrial cities. Many came from rural areas or small towns. While county officers and WLA representatives were upper- or upper-middle class, and many of them were propertied, most of the young women who volunteered to work on the land, the rank-and-file, tended to be from middle or working-class backgrounds. There were a few upper-class young recruits as Hazel King, 83, who joined the Land Army in 1943 as a tractor driver, remembered:

> We had some upper-class girls working on the tractors; well one went into the office and one was an assistant foreman but the majority of girls were like myself, working class, but we had all sorts. When we were in the hostel we had a trainee chiropodist, she was called up, she used to do our feet for us because our feet did ache.

In her history of the WLA, Vita Sackville West wrote that land girls were:

> ...by the very nature of their occupation rural, not urban. Yet often in her previous occupation she has been urban enough. She has been a shop assistant, a manicurist, a hair-dresser, a shorthand-typist, a ballet-dancer, a milliner, a mannequin, a saleswoman, an insurance clerk. She has worn silk stockings and high-heeled shoes, pretty frocks and jaunty hats; has had plenty of fun, being young and gay; has done her job during the working hours, and then at the end of the day has returned to her personal life among friends or family, entertainment or home...

Whether land girls had enjoyed plenty of fun before or not, most of the new recruits had already been in the labour force before volunteering for the WLA. Phyllis Cole, 87, who worked as a thresher in and around Uckfield, had previously worked in a bakery, then in Boots the chemist before being called up. Joan Markby, 85, who lived in Bournemouth and whose mother did not think she would be able to cope with the rigours of outdoor life, had been a secretary for a firm of accountants when she joined up. Others had been typists, clerks, milliners, beauticians, or even mannequins, modelling hats or dresses in department stores in London or large towns.

Many of the young women, particularly those from rural areas, had left school and gone straight into domestic service. Eileen Hodd, who described herself as 'just a country girl', came from Sandhurst in Kent. She left school when she was 14, and went into service, working in the 'big house' for about two years, then came out of service and joined the Land Army. Barbara Giles, 85, joined the Land Army in Kent when she was just coming up for 17. She, too, had gone into service as a 'tween maid' helping in the house and the kitchen then, following a

> ....Members of the Land Army have proved their intelligence by joining the Land Army. Coming from every profession and calling, they have all realised what is the most important job they can do today...
>
> (The *Land Girl*, April 1940, first issue)

road accident, took a job in Sainsbury's before becoming a land girl. Helen Dawson left school aged 14, went into service and worked as a parlour maid for a local doctor before becoming a land girl, as did Blanche Lucas who worked in service in Brightling after leaving school.

The range of previous occupations was quite extensive and land girls often found themselves working alongside young women from very different jobs. In June 1940, the *Land Girl* magazine included an article that had been sent in from five land girls working on a farm in the West Riding of Yorkshire, who described their previous occupations as 'dog breeding, domestic science, secretarial work and librarianship'.

Civilians and Volunteers

One thing that all members of the WLA had in common was that they were civilians: despite its name, the WLA always was a civilian organization. Women were employed by farmers rather than by the state and were not subject to the same discipline as women in the armed forces which, for some, was its attraction. However, civilian status had pros and cons: while the land girls did not have to abide by the strict rules and regulations imposed on their sisters in the armed forces – only the farmer had the right to hire or fire although the WLA itself recruited and could also dismiss land girls – equally they had less protection and none of the automatic benefits enjoyed by forces women, such as clothing allowances or clubs for relaxation, something that Lady Denman and her colleagues worked hard to change.

Most of the women who joined the Land Army were young, in their teens or early twenties, and by far the greatest majority were volunteers, who did not wait to be directed into essential work but chose the Land Army in preference to other areas of war work. A few had considered some of the other women's auxiliary services, such as the ATS or WRNS, but most wanted to work on the land. Their reasons varied considerably. There was a war on and they wanted to get involved and 'do their bit' for the war effort but, apart from patriotism, there were other reasons too. For some, joining the Land Army meant an opportunity to leave home for the first time, away from some of the restrictions that home life could mean.

For Margaret Donaldson, 84, joining the Land Army meant leaving home, and the chance to work in the country. She came from a large family; her mother had 10 children, and lived in Heston, not far from where London airport is now situated. She left school and worked in a shop, a stationers and confectioners, and learned sub-post office work. It was around the time of the Battle of Britain and she remembers cycling to work, and seeing the dogfights overhead. Shortly after the Battle of Britain, in 1940, she joined the Land Army:

> I wanted a change. I wanted to get away from home. I loved the open air, so that's why I decided. It's all a bit vague now. When I used to cycle to work past fields and see people working in them, I used to think how lovely to do that, being out in the fresh air...I've always loved fresh air and that's what made me get into it. There must have been an application place but it's a bit vague now. We didn't have any checks but I've got a feeling I must have gone to the labour exchange, it wasn't about being involved in war work, I just wanted to work on the land. I joined and I was posted to a place called Coddenham in East Suffolk.

Land girls could be sent anywhere in the country, and had to agree to this when they joined. However, not all women wanted to leave home and some were actually recruited locally. Eileen Hodd, for instance, volunteered for the Land Army for the simple reason that:

> My sister worked for the same farmer as the farm we lived on and my father worked for that farmer and my sister joined the Land Army and he [the farmer] applied for her so she stayed at home. She married and I decided I would join the Land Army so I volunteered and Chris, my boss said, 'If you join, I will apply for you because I need another hand,' so I still lived at home.

Many women were reluctant to leave home or to be moved around the country and, in fact, although the WLA was set up as a mobile force and land girls could be, and were, sent all over the country, organizers and recruitment officers always tried to place volunteers in their own county as a first option. Some young women, particularly those from rural areas, joined the Land Army so they could remain as close as possible to home. This later caused resentment from women in other services, but there were often good reasons for staying close to home, such as elderly or sick parents, or maybe just fear of the unknown.

Blanche Lucas, who joined the Land Army in 1942 did so 'because I didn't want to go away from home, particularly a long way away from home to go in the services, like the WRNS or the army, and I think the next thing would have been, like some girls did, the munitions factories. I could never have stood being indoors, I'm too much of an outdoor person, always lived on a farm with animals, and I knew the farmers around and I could almost choose where I went rather than be sent.

> A farmer asked his new Land Girl what breed of cows she had milked in her last job. She said she had no idea. The farmer suggested they might have been 'Shorthorns'. 'Oh no' was the answer, 'they all had long horns!'
>
> (The *Land Girl*, October 1940)

Helen Dawson, too, was reluctant to leave home. She was working for a doctor in Dallington, who wanted her to stay on, but she was keen to do her bit for the war effort. Her first choice had been the ATS but 'they said no, they wanted land girls, so they persuaded me in the end, also my mother was a widow and I didn't want to go away and my first position, after I had been to college, was in Dallington so I was with my mother.'

Hazel King was recruited locally by people she knew. She had worked in service and then in a garage in Rye before she joined the Land Army:

All the young men were called up, they needed a garage lad, so he suggested I went and next door there was a place called the Bonding Store and that's where they had a Land Army depot. I just volunteered. The man in charge of the depot used to come round the garage for different things and he used to say, 'When are you going to come and join us?' I was rather tempted because, apart from anything else,

I liked the uniform and I've always liked the outdoor life and I thought about it and my mum said 'Well, it's up to you' and my particular friend, she was younger than me, and I, we went to Hastings and we volunteered. She put her age up because they weren't that fussy in those days. I was 18; well I was 18 in the September. I don't exactly remember when we volunteered but I know I started work on 10 May 1943. We had to go to the Hastings Employment Office to sign on, actually there were four Rye girls.

Personal reasons often underpinned choice. One former land girl, who was extremely shy, was involved with an unwanted boyfriend; rather than pluck up the courage to end the relationship, she solved the problem by joining the Land Army and was sent away. Phyllis Cole also had personal and rather tragic reasons for joining. She was about 20 when she joined up and already a young widow. Her husband had died, falling from a tree while putting up communications wire; he had not even had time to go abroad. Shortly afterwards she was called up:

I was pleased because I was walking over the marshes, Romney Marshes, and looking at the planes and hoping they would bomb me, I was so young and hopeless, so going into the Land Army was my way of putting things back. You were called up and that's what you do and I couldn't go and let my husband down.

Many would-be land girls were attracted by the idea of working in the countryside, and the joy of being in the open air, often in preference to the enclosed and dangerous work of the munitions, although young women from towns and cities who dreamed of a romantic country life based on images in recruitment posters, often got quite a nasty shock when they encountered the harsh reality of farming for the first time. Eileen Grabham, a Londoner from Shoreditch, was one who joined the Land Army 'because I always loved the country and because of the uniform, which was attractive. But mostly I joined because I loved the country.' There were many others who shared her sentiments.

An Attractive Uniform

A surprising number of recruits were attracted by the Land Army uniform, which was considered by some to be quite stylish, and by others as quite odd. Lady Denman felt strongly that the Land Army deserved its own uniform and, in fact, employed a fashion designer to produce the Land Army greatcoat, which was almost universally admired. It was important to Lady Denman and the WLA officials that the land girls should be seen to be part of a uniformed service, even if they were civilians.

Reflecting the healthy outdoor life of the land girl, the 'walking out' uniform included laced brown brogues, brown corduroy breeches, knee length fawn socks, and a green V-necked long sleeved pullover, which was worn over a fawn aertex shirt, topped by a brown slouch hat. The hat alone was a source of much discussion and frustration, as land girls often wore their hats in a variety of ways, while the WLA insisted it should be worn squarely on the head. On being accepted into the Land Army, land girls were entitled to a certain amount of clothing, for which they handed over clothing coupons, and could buy a Land Army tie, something some land girls resented, feeling they should not have to pay for it. There was also a distinctive WLA badge, showing a wheat sheaf, topped by a crown. Not surprisingly working clothes were more functional and included gumboots, long white coats and dungarees.

Most land girls had quite strong views about their uniform, and the public, too, was somewhat bemused at first. At the start of the war clothing supplies were fairly random and early recruits were not immediately kitted out with everything they needed, although the process of supplying uniforms became more efficient as time went on. Clothes did not always fit and the heavy shoes were hard on feet unaccustomed to that sort of footwear. Peggy Pearce, who joined the Land Army at the beginning of the war, was rather surprised at the uniform and remembered travelling by train from London with her friend, both of them wearing their Land Army uniforms:

Oh, it was a scream the uniform. We went by train from

Forest Hill and then we changed. It was heavy brown shoes, long socks, thick long socks and jodhpurs and there were two long-sleeved shirts and two short-sleeved shirts and a green pullover and a hat and that was all, no overcoats, nothing like that. We had two drill coats, which you wore out in the field; if you were a bit chilly, you put the drill coat on. You had no great overcoat, not for many years and we didn't have Wellington boots. When we sat in the train we heard one or two people saying, 'What are they?' You'd have thought we might have looked like something going onto the land wouldn't you? 'Who are they?' 'What are they doing?' It was funny; the people in the carriage didn't know about Land Girls.

One of the things that characterized the Land Army uniform was that it meant wearing trousers, which was practical but in the 1940s it was a new experience for many of the new recruits. Some welcomed them, others took longer to get used to the idea. Helen Dawson thought the uniform was 'funny' and viewed the trousers with some suspicion:

Well, at first, gosh, women's breeches but then you got used to it. I've never worn trousers much; I feel happier in a skirt. It did feel odd and of course we had the ordinary khaki overalls with a bib and a long jacket like the auctioneers wear, when you were working.

Blanche Lucas also would have preferred something more feminine:

It wasn't very elegant. It was smart in its way and they were good clothes…a lovely big coat, it was used at home for years after, it never wore out. We had very nice thick brown shoes, which looked nice, and stockings and corduroy jodhpurs and a green jumper and a shirt, and for work we had dungarees. I hadn't worn trousers before. I'm not a trouser sort of person but well you had to. The breeches were more for dressing up, outings and things like that. I can't say I liked it. Had there been something more feminine,

I would have been happy to wear it but it was the Land Army uniform and one accepted it.

By contrast, there were others who appreciated the trousers. Eileen Hodd was one who did:

I liked it. I'm a trouser girl anyway. In the wintertime you had breeches that came just below the knee and long socks and living in the country, I'd always had good leather lace-up shoes so they weren't hard for me because we lived down the lane on the farm, we never had flimsy shoes, and green Wellingtons you were supplied with. In the summer you had overalls, you had a long-sleeved poplin shirt in the winter to wear with breeches and a green sweater, V-necked green sweater and a green tie for when you went out. In the summer you had dungaree beige overalls and aertex beige short-sleeved shirts and if you wore it out you could apply for more.

As in the First World War, however, there were some, including parents and husbands, who regarded women wearing trousers as anathema. Bernice Birch, from Kent, who was 20 when she joined up, remembered that her mother:

...didn't think we should wear trousers. I hadn't worn them before, and I was 20. She was all right afterwards. My husband wasn't. 'Girls wearing trousers,' he was absolutely disgusted.

As well as trousers, many land girls found their sturdy shoes could only be described as 'clodhoppers'.

A green felt armband with the letters WLA embroidered in red completed the uniform and for every six months' service, land girls were sent a small diamond-shaped piece of material that they sewed onto their armbands. After two years' service, the diamonds formed a square, so length of service was immediately apparent.

Sticking To It

The Land Army was one of the most popular of the wartime

services but acceptance was not necessarily automatic. According to the *Land Girl* (October 1940), out of every 12 women, who expressed an interest in joining the Land Army, sometimes only one was actually suitable. Women had to be of strong 'physique', although physical examinations were often cursory, and had to be prepared to commit themselves to the Land Army for the duration of the war, unless exceptional circumstances prevented them from doing so.

> Lady Somebody's daughter joined up too because she'd got a horse [but] she didn't last five minutes. They didn't like the hard work.
>
> (Peggy Pearce)

From the outset, organizers in the Land Army stressed the need for land girls to 'stick to the job', and not to give up. As war continued and the need for land girls became more urgent, this message got stronger, particularly as the first wave of land girls proved their worth. In January 1941, the *Land Girl* magazine drove the message home, in an editorial advising older members to give help, support and encouragement to new recruits, pointing out that:

> ...every new volunteer costs the country a substantial sum of money for her training, equipment and incidental expenses. If she gives up, she represents a dead loss, and the country cannot afford dead losses...

Little Previous Experience

Having been accepted for the Land Army, the new land girls were issued with their uniforms, given some training, if necessary, either in a college or on a training farm, then sent to wherever they were to work, either in their own county or elsewhere. Some recruits already had some farming experience or knowledge of the countryside. Those who came from country areas had often done seasonal work, fruit or hop picking, or helping with the harvest. Beryl Peacham had grown up on a farm, so the work held few surprises for her. She was not given any training because, they said, 'Well, you know more than most' and a farming friend of hers who lived on a nearby farm was specifically asked to join the Land Army to help young women, such as shop workers, make the transition to working on the land. Eileen Hodd did not have any training either: 'I was a country girl anyway so I just sort of went into work in the fields, it was very mixed farming, it was corn and hay, hops, fruit, cows, sheep, there was a carter, there was a shepherd…just

To All Land Girls
From an admirer of their work

I saw a Land Girl working
Alone in an open field.
Her hard, once elegant hands
A Stalwart hoe did wield.
Her back was bent as she slew the weeds
That spoiled the potatoes' growth;
She never wilted, she never paused,
She had taken her silent oath.

At last the day was nearly done,
The sun was sinking low;
She gathered up her jacket
Then slowly cleaned her hoe.
She passed the chair where I sat
(I am feeble in body and sight).
She smiled at me as she said:
'Been hot to-day. Good-night.'

We hear the valiant deeds of our men in
'furrin parts,'
Deeds which bring the tears to our eyes, a
glow of pride to our hearts –
But when the war is over and peace at last
restored,
I shall always remember the Land Girl, who
made her hoe her sword.

(The *Land Girl*, July 1940)

an average farm, not huge.'

Many of the new recruits, particularly those from towns and cities, or women who had left the countryside to work in towns, knew little or nothing at all about farming; some had never even encountered a cow, let alone tried to milk one, and very few town dwellers had any real idea of the backbreaking work in store for them. Joan Markby, for instance, was 'frightened of cows, terrified, I wouldn't go near them, then we got sent to this month's training, and I got to know the cows'.

In May 1940, the *Land Girl* commented that 'many who came into the Land Army had little previous experience, if any', not just of tackling a whole range of unfamiliar and unusual tasks, but also of getting up at crack of dawn, suffering stiff muscles, chilblains, chapped lips, cracked fingers, blistered hands, wet clothes and a range of other problems and discomforts. Blanche Lucas remembered that arriving on the land was particularly difficult for urban young women:

> Some girls came from the north and they were hairdressers and all sorts, and of course London, a lot came to this area, East and West Sussex and [it was strange for them] never having had any experience of the hard work which they put their hand to, which is why the farmers said, at the outbreak of war 'they'll never manage it, they'll never do a man's job'.

Vita Sackville-West summed up the situation in her book *The Women's Land Army*:

> ...Perhaps she [the land girl] didn't always know how hard the life was going to be. Perhaps she had visions of herself teaching gentle little calves to suck her finger in a bucket of milk. She came...in many instances from a very different kind of life, scarcely knowing, as country people say, 'one end of a cow from the other'. It was all very well for the country-born girls, who did at least know what they were going into...The town-bred girl didn't always know. Her idea of the country was a summer-holiday idea, when you strolled down a Hampshire lane picking wildflowers...or lay in the sun on the Sussex Downs sniffing the thyme and gorse...

Jokes and Ridicule

It was hardly surprising then that land girls were often the subject of ridicule and the butt of jokes. It was generally assumed, particularly by farmers, that the new recruits would be unable to find their way around a cow, or distinguish sugar beets from weeds, and would arrive for work seeing farming life through a rosy-tinted image of cuddly lambs and fluffy chickens. There were plenty of cartoons and jokes to this effect, not least in the pages of the *Land Girl* magazine, which sensibly chose to include jokes, cartoons and humorous articles about land girls and their early mistakes. At the beginning of the war, farmers often viewed the new land girls, arriving on their farms, with a sense of horror and foreboding. Practical jokes were commonplace, and some could turn nasty, even though they were not intended to do so. Margaret Donaldson was at the receiving end of a practical joke that nearly had serious consequences:

> She volunteered,
> She volunteered to be a Land Girl!
> Ten bob a week,
> Nothing much to eat,
> Great big boots,
> And blisters on her feet.
> If it wasn't for the war,
> She'd be where she was before.
> Land Girl - You're barmy!
>
> (Land Army song)

Mostly the cows were very good and they knew their own places and we just put their little chains on before we got the water to wash their udders but on one occasion, this one cow went down the gangway between the stalls, which is where we used to put their feed in, and I said to the cowmen, 'What shall I do' and they said 'Oh, just push her back, push her back' but when she got to the end where there was a step up, I said 'Now what shall I do?' and they said 'Oh, get hold of her leg' and [I did] and of course the other [leg] came up and hit me in the face, and the next morning I appeared with a lovely black eye and they were all laughing; they knew I should never have got hold of a cow's leg at the back. They all had a good laugh at my expense.

Like many inexperienced land girls, who had come from towns and cities, Margaret also found some aspects of farming embarrassing:

> Sometimes when I was working in the dairy, the kitchen staff would come through and say we'd had permission to watch the bull siring the cow, but I was too embarrassed to go and watch. They could, they were country people, but I didn't like to.

Not surprisingly some parents were sorry to see their daughters choosing the Land Army for their war service, although this did not stop determined would-be land girls, some of whom joined up against their parents' wishes. One land girl, Pamela McDowell, originally wanted to join the WRNS. Having had some farm experience, however – she had worked on her uncle's farm – the authorities suggested that she join the Land Army instead. Her mother was completely opposed to the idea on the grounds that farming people were rough and 'not the sort of people that her daughter should associate with'. In the event Pamela joined the Land Army in London and was sent to a farm in Maidstone. Apparently her mother never came to terms with her daughter's decision.

Within a very short space of time, however, the inexperienced land girls were tackling just about every job that was thrown at them and, by 1943, they were helping to produce some 70 per cent of the nation's food.

Mrs Blanche Lucas

Taken from a biographical piece that Blanche wrote for her local
Aviation Society who were producing a history of Etchingham, Sussex.

In 1942 I volunteered for the Women's Land Army (in spite of having
to be mobile and prepared to go anywhere in the country). I was able to
work on a dairy and arable farm near home, and preferred the healthy
lifestyle.

It was hard work and long hours during the summer months, but we
had fun. There were rallies and we would put on a variety show for the
local people.

I started on one farm and was billeted nearby with a girl called Peggy
with whom I still correspond. I cycled everywhere, and at 6.30 a.m. the
air was lovely and fresh, and cobwebs would brush across my face.

Often I did not have to walk far to bring in the cows for milking. They
knew the call and would come to the gate and follow me. At the outset it
was hand milking and a few of the Friesians kicked, on one occasion I
landed in the gutter - very painful!

After the milking session the cows were turned out and it was off to
the fields to do general farm work, hoeing, hedging and some reclamation. I learnt to drive a tractor, one had to stop to change gear and they
ran on a product called TVO (tractor vaporizing oil). I also tried my
hand at thatching and dung spreading, but this was not a pleasant job.
Root lifting and trimming swedes could be very mucky and it was doing
this I cut a thumb and will carry the scar for the rest of my life - no
thoughts of compensation then!

I then left to work on another farm, 'Pearch Hill', where I lived in with
the family, who were a happy bunch. Our dining table doubled as a
shelter which, when the siren sounded, we were supposed to get under. I
hated the idea of being buried alive and preferred to be outside to watch

the action. We had radio for amusement but no television. For the girls' supper, the lady of the house would put on the range stove a large saucepan of milk and when hot, add bread and sugar, and it was delicious. The menfolk had OXO.

German POWs came from a nearby camp to help out with haymaking. In the evenings we found it more profitable to help out a neighbouring farmer, and at the end of the evening's work we would enjoy a drink with a piece or two of bread pudding, homemade of course.

Harvesting I enjoyed, and nearing the end of the field, rabbits would scamper all ways and it was great fun running to catch them before they reached the fence. They were also part of a staple diet in those days. Following behind the binder we made stooks of six or eight sheaves of corn to dry, these were then loaded on to a wagon with a pitchfork. Sometimes we took a turn on the wagon. At times the local firemen helped for a few hours, one of them called Alec Duck who had cultivated a rather portly stature provided a soft landing pad for us coming down off the wagon. Then it was time for the thrasher to move in, this was a nasty, dusty job, raking away the chaff.

When the doodlebugs started to come over we were issued with tin helmets, a guard against bullets from aircraft trying to bring them down.

In 1946 I left the WLA to help on my brother-in-law's farm, And they thought women could not do a man's job in wartime!

Given the same set of circumstances, I would do it all over again - minus the kicking cow!

* * *

Chapter 5

Working on the Land

The versatility of the Land Army is astonishing...skilled hairdressers find themselves combing cows' tails, beauty specialists cut corn, children's nurses feed and comfort calves, shop assistants count carrots, housemaids sweep out farmyards and typists hoe endless rows.

(The *Land Girl*, October 1940)

NO MATTER what they had been doing before, land girls turned their hands to just about every type of farming job imaginable. At the start of the war, some land girls were underemployed and mainly involved in seasonal work. But, as war continued, the demand for labour intensified, and land girls were soon fully occupied. They were employed in general farming and in more specialized areas. They worked as dairymaids; they worked with horses, sheep, pigs and poultry; they were used for hedging, ditching, thatching, threshing and harvesting. They learned to drive and operate tractors and combine harvesters, and were used to kill rats. They toiled on large and small farms, in gangs or on their own; they worked as fruit pickers, on market gardens and in greenhouses. And, from 1942, thousands of land girls worked in the Women's Timber Corps. The work was hard and exhausting; the pay was poor, the hours were long and conditions were often primitive – most of the work had to be done by hand – but, thanks to the land girls, harvests were brought in, fruit and vegetables were produced, and thousands of acres were laid down to arable crops that formed the basis of the British wartime diet.

An Impressive List

In her book *The Women's Land Army*, Vita Sackville-West provided an overview of a land girl's work:

> She milks; she does general farm-work, which includes ploughing, weeding, hoeing, dung-spreading, lifting and clamping potatoes and other root crops, brishing and laying hedges, cleaning ditches, haymaking, harvesting, threshing; in more specialised ways, she prunes and sprays fruit-trees, picks and packs the fruit, makes and lays thatch, makes silage, pulls flax, destroys rats, works an excavator, reclaims bad land, works in commercial gardens and private gardens, works in the forests felling timber, measuring timber; planting young trees…

It was quite an impressive list and by no means comprehensive. The *Land Army Manual*, a handbook for members of the WLA, which was published in 1941, listed the types of work that new recruits might expect to do: forestry work; milk rounds; fruit growing, including pruning, spraying, cultivation, fruit thinning and marketing; market gardening, growing vegetables for market, including preparing the ground and sewing the seed by hand or mechanically, hoeing along rows, picking peas, pulling carrots and so on; glasshouse work, cultivating food crops such as cucumbers, lettuce, tomatoes, and radishes. The list continued to include dairy farming, poultry farming, including care of hens, chickens, and 'the fluffy little chicks to look after', ducks, geese and maybe turkeys; tractor driving – volunteers were not expected to be first-class mechanics but were advised to study the handbook and to know general maintenance; sheep farming, and general farming. Interestingly, there was no reference to rat catching or other forms of pest control, and the descriptions of the work were fairly bland: they rarely touched on the gritty reality.

WLA officials stressed that land girls were not domestic workers: they were outdoor workers, engaged in producing the nation's food and Land Army representatives came down heavily on any farmers who tried to use land girls for domestic tasks. In her book *Land Girl*, Anne Hall, who spent six years in the WLA, describes how, at her first posting, the farmer's wife expected her to work around the house, chop wood and do the washing up. She sent a letter complaining about the situation to her local WLA rep and was moved to another farm.

Training

Recruits who had no previous farming experience, and there were many of them, were offered training on a training farm or centre, an agricultural college or farm institute. Volunteers who were trained on a farm might continue their employment there or more usually be sent to another farm. Those who had some experience were sent directly into 'vital employment'.

Many inexperienced land girls, however, were just placed on farms and expected to pick up the work, learning as they went along. Sheelah Cruttenden's children recollect that their mother was just 'thrown in at the deep end' and, in her written account, she says she 'was offered no training and tasks were either commonsense or learnt on the job, from fellow land girls'. WLA officials expected that farmers would take the time and trouble to teach land girls, which often happened, but sometimes it did not and land girls had to learn the work through trial and error.

The WLA encouraged land girls to take every opportunity to develop their skills and inform themselves about farming. Land girls were urged to attend any classes or demonstrations that were organized in their area, such as tractor driving, or ploughing. They could do correspondence courses and the *Land Girl* regularly featured articles on topics such as how to drive and maintain a tractor, how to clean cowsheds, including the need to remove manure and soiled litter, brushing down walls and lime washing; how to clean cows, which included curry combing flanks and tail, brushing the cows hindquarters using a slightly damp brush, washing the udder, and wiping the teats. The whole operation, it was said, should only take a few minutes. There were also articles on horticulture, sterilizing, how to keep poultry, fruit cultivation, and how to identify different plants and bird life. Farming programmes on the radio were listed and the magazine included quizzes with questions such as 'How do (a) horses and (b) cows get up from a recumbent position?', 'How many gallons of milk will a good ordinary cow give in a year?' and 'How many stomachs has a cow?' Quite how much time busy and exhausted land girls had for listening to radio or answering general knowledge questions is probably debatable.

> I'd never really met up with a cow before, never seen cows before, and the first thing we had to learn was to wash their backsides and their udder and that was a bit of a shock; I was a little bit frightened of them. Some were all right, some were spiteful, they used to swish you around the face with their tails; I had one tread on my toe once. The woman who was teaching us, [said] we had to learn milking to the tune of 'Good King Wenceslas'. It's a good job it wasn't 'In the Mood'.
>
> (Eileen Grabham)

Helen Dawson did about six weeks' training in dairy farming at a college, with other recruits, some of whom were Londoners who apparently found the work very strange, and was then sent to work on a farm in Bodiam. Her home overlooks the fields that she worked in during the war:

I went to the college. There were several girls and we all slept in a dormitory or big room and we used to have to get up at 4 o'clock in the morning and look after the cows. There were 20 cows down one side and down the other and there was this wooden thing with an udder made of rubber and you had to sit down and learn to press and pull. I could still milk a cow now. A lot of girls didn't milk them because they had machines; I never worked with machines, we [hand] milked them. We came in at 8 o'clock for our breakfast and was I hungry! I loved the cows, except one, Blackie, she used to kick, she knocked me over, their tails would switch round so you tied them to their legs, they'd got mess all over, and they'd swing round and it would hurt, painful but it's marvellous how they all know where to go and if you try to switch them round and put them in a different compartment, they'll still keep trying to go where they want, they know where to go.

When I did get on the farm, the first job I had was in those fields [pointing out of the window], stacking or stooking up corn because you stooked them up then, they were in sheaves, and then I was general really because I did hay making, milking the cows, feeding the pigs and chickens, picking the apples. I think I got to work about half-past seven, milked the cows and then I would go out with the horse and cart, throwing dung out along the roads. I used to drive a tractor, and worked with the horses, harrowing and that. I couldn't lift up the shaft to put the horse in, I needed help; they were heavy. You had to reverse the horse back in. We finished about 5 o'clock in the evening, if you didn't have to work overtime doing haymaking or something. Then I worked on a kitchen farm [doing] general farming, milking, harrowing, hay harvesting, then there was hop-picking. I used to bring the milk up to the school, they were open buckets then and I used to bring them up on my bicycle when I came up for breakfast. [I also] made butter, it was always Saturday mornings, and you had to turn the handle and sometimes it wouldn't turn and you wanted to get off and it wouldn't turn.

It is an old saying that an army marches on its stomach. Nowadays it is the whole nation, not only the army, that fights a war, and nothing is more important than the care of the nation's food... This is the Land Army's particular job...

(The *Land Girl* April 1940)

Margaret Donaldson was sent to a farm in Ipswich, where she did three weeks' training in dairy work:

It was just a farm, not a college. They stuck me under a very gentle cow so if you were nervous it didn't budge. After that I was posted to a place called Coddenham, in East Suffolk. I used to cycle to work. In the summer across the fields it was lovely, you had to break all the cobwebs, past a lot of army men, just rubbing their eyes and getting up. I had to be there at 5, an early start but we didn't have to round up any of the cows because they were all waiting impatiently to get milked, so you just opened the gates and they headed into the cowsheds themselves. I was working on a general farm, it had lots of fields, but it was primarily dairy and we used to milk the cows. Some of us took it in turns to put the machines on one day, and the rest of us would strip the

At a Farm Institute one trainee told the cowman that she had 'emptied' her cow – at least she could not get any more out of the corners.

(The *Land Girl* March 1941)

cows afterwards [completing the milking]. I'd seen cows but didn't know anything about them. The farmer was quite nice, he wasn't too bad and he had a very pleasant wife, she was a working wife; she used to work along with us during the harvesting, which of course was a long day. We used to work until nightfall.

After doing the milking, Margaret had to:

...clean out the cowsheds and sterilise the equipment. After that we had some breakfast, a big mug of tea and a good lump of bread and cheese [and] after breakfast we had to go down to the fields. It depended on the time of year: if it was summer there would be hay making and harvesting but if it wasn't, then we did mangel pulling, which is cattle feed and then of course after lunch, which was about 2.30-3.00, we'd have to come and have the milking session again. I was working seven days a week; we got one weekend off in three. One job I didn't like was cutting down thistles, we had scythes and had to slice them as low as we could, it only went on for a few hours but it was a job that I really didn't like.

Heavy Work

While some land girls worked in dairies, others collected and delivered milk. It was heavy work. Barbara Giles drove a motorbike and sidecar, delivering milk over a wide area of Kent. She did not receive any training but:

...went straight to the farm and picked it up as we went along. They took us out driving, taught us how to drive and the same with the farm, the farm workers showed you what to do. I collected churns one day, the other time I was out delivering the milk all round the area, driving a motorbike and sidecar. I lifted the churns all by myself and loaded the motorbike up with four pints, two pints, pints and half pints.

It was hard work. In fact after I was married and when I had my first baby, I had rather a bad time and they said to me it was because my muscles were so hard because I had been doing a man's job.

(Hazel King)

Other land girls had to roll heavy milk churns from the dairies out into the road or heave them onto lorries. For those who were already toughened up, it was not always too arduous but for those who had come straight from office or shop jobs, it took time for aching muscles and backs to become accustomed to the constant bending and lifting that formed part of the land girl's daily routine.

One former land girl, Marge, from mid-Wales, who was sent to Warwickshire, remembered:

Picking potatoes in clamps, we used to have to riddle them in winter to get the small ones out and then go through and then we used to have to pile them in boxes, because the fields used to get waterlogged. The lorry used to come into the field and once it was loaded up it couldn't get off the field so we used to have to park it in the road and then put planks across the dykes and we used to have to carry these full sacks of potatoes on our backs across these planks and load the lorry up. We didn't think it was hard work...it had to be done and that was that.

Despite the rigours of the work she never regretted joining the Land Army.

Joan Markby did a month's training in mixed farming and dairy work during which she was sent around to different farms in Dorset. She also learned to drive a tractor, knocking over a gatepost during the process, one of the very few mistakes she made. After her training, she was sent first to a farm in Landford and then to another in Maiden Newton, near Dorchester, where she was mainly working with cows and pigs but, like other land girls, she also worked in the fields, cutting kale, haymaking and planting potatoes:

> We had two, what I call old men; they were old because they stayed on the farm and they were very nice. They called us 'maid' and I remember when we were planting potatoes, I was going along dropping the potatoes in and the old man said 'Very well maid, but they won't jump up to meet you when you go back'. He meant that I had to bend down, I was just dropping them in, I wasn't bending down and putting them in, and he said 'Well, they won't jump up to meet you when you come back to pick them', so I had to bend down then.

Farming could take its toll on the body. One job that Peggy Pearce disliked intensely was working in watercress beds:

> I went to Mitcham in Surrey. I didn't like it but I had to go to watercress beds and then in the winter mustard and cress greenhouses. We had to cut the watercress and put it into bunches, into a wooden box and when it was full, we had to walk over the water, we had a plank, and you couldn't see where you were going and we'd got this great heavy box. I fell in more than once, no wonder I'm riddled with arthritis. It was very, very hard and even with the mustard and cress, you had a knife and you had to cut some and put it in a punnet till it was absolutely full. I loved the farming, I wasn't keen on the watercress.

Filthy, Dirty Work

By general consensus, threshing was one of the hardest jobs on the farm and it could be absolutely filthy. Land girls were not given protective clothing, nor were gloves much use; some girls covered their faces and hair with scarves for the dirtiest work. Phyllis Cole worked in the Uckfield area as one of a gang of land girls who were sent out to different farms to do threshing. She did not have any training:

I was threshing. It is really hard work. No training but the people on the farms, as you went around the farms, they told you exactly what to do. They positioned you. They said, there are four positions: up on the top [of the stack] and when you're up there, you cut the strings and there's a man opposite you threading it into the machine, and then there's someone on the stack, who is throwing down the sheaves and then there's somebody out the back who's doing the cavings, and then another on along the side. The man takes it [threshing machine] up to the stacks, they used to have stacks then, lovely big stacks, shame you don't see them today, you position it up to the end of it and then you can have a man and a girl on the top and when you take the thatching off and you've got a pitchfork and he's got a pitchfork and he throws them down onto the machine and it's got a great long hopper, and you've got a girl there. Usually what they wanted you to do was pick the sack up, hold the knot and cut it, and then you had a great big gaping hole there with the rubbish. The cavings were the worst because all the dirt and filth comes out; it's where it [thresher] shakes all the stuff and one lot is the straw. The farmer stands there with the sacks, then he takes the sack off, ties it up and puts another sack on, that's the cleanest part but when you get a bit further along, then you've got all this dust and stuff. We didn't wear any protective clothing, only dungarees. We couldn't wear gloves but our hands got hardened. That was my work the whole time I was in the Land Army. It was very, very, very hard. Your hands were rough, you couldn't wear gloves, it was hard [and] it was dirty work but you had fun too.

Land girls were expected to do any task given to them, so even if they had been trained in specific jobs, such as dairying, they would be expected to work with threshers and help with haymaking. Margaret Donaldson remembered the dirt involved:

We used to do stacking, fork up the sheaves and someone on top would do the stacking. I was one time called the 'chaff boy', when we were getting the grain out, that was a filthy job, you used to get as black as anything, it came down the hopper and I had to bag it up, the dirtiest job you could get. It's amazing, you see this lovely golden corn but you don't realise how dirty it can get.

Dirt was not the only problem: working in the fields during wintertime was gruelling and Land Army clothing did not always offer much protection. Many women put long johns under their clothes – one woman borrowed some from one of the men on her farm; many tried to pile jerseys on top of each other and others even wore their formal greatcoats against the cold.

Working with Tractors

Many land girls learned to drive tractors during the war. Tractors then were primitive and uncomfortable, with seats taken off in case of accidents, so if a land girl drove into a ditch, which happened fairly frequently, she could get off safely. Hazel King volunteered for the Land Army in 1943 and, with her friend Mavis, joined the small army of tractor girls who were ploughing up Romney Marsh for use as arable land. She had not even driven a car before:

All I could ride was a bike, so it was new to us. We had six weeks' training in what they called the tractor school and were shown the ins and outs of sparking plugs, how to start and how to stop. Mind you, tractors were very basic in those days. We started off here [in Rye] then they moved it up to Staplecross and then the whole school moved up there and we lived in a hostel in Northiam for about six weeks and cycled to work every day. By that time we knew about engines and things and then we were taught ploughing and after we were proficient in ploughing, we moved back to Rye and down onto the marsh. I think we started work at eight o'clock and then we finished about half past five, six o'clock, but of course in the summer, because it was double summer time, we were sometimes there at nine o'clock at night. We had the foreman and a couple of engineers because we were about 30 girls, all tractor drivers. We worked for the East Sussex Royal Agricultural Committee and we had land all down the marsh and on Winchelsea Beach, I don't know how many thousands of acres, they had already started ploughing in and we carried on. We were ploughing up Romney Marsh because it had been all sheep, and we ploughed it up and put it down to corn and arable. I loved ploughing, I really did. I shouldn't say it myself, but I became quite a champion. On the whole we worked on our own because if you were on the tractor, there would be other girls in the field doing the same sort of thing because they were big fields but apart from break times, mid-morning and lunch time, we didn't see much of each other.

There were one or two tips into the ditch if you weren't careful and once, when I was backing the tractor for the girl to fit, I don't know what it was that I was going to have on the plough, I got her fingers caught. It was very repetitive doing the ploughing until we got it perfect and that's how we came to have the accidents in the ditches; as you keep going round the earth gets so high and you've got to come out and turn and it doesn't always turn round and you end up with the tractor in the ditch and that's a bit scary. But we never lost anybody. I landed in the ditch a couple of times but Margery went right down into the ditch. We always got out all right. I didn't mind getting on the tractor and being towed out but it was a bit hazardous.

In the morning we had to start those tractors and it was damned hard work on a cold morning. You must keep your thumb behind the handle otherwise you might break it. One day a couple of us were reaping a field and we must have got too close to the hedge, we disturbed a wild bees' nest in the hedge, so we had to strip in the field because we were covered in bees.

Like others, Hazel had to do plenty of other jobs, including threshing, working on the roads, and growing potatoes and sugar beet on Romney Marsh; like most land girls, she was often given the dirtiest work:

We used to have to help on the thresher; there was a threshing gang that came around. We got all the dirty jobs at the end, with all the dust. The corn was still in its ears then, it went through the thresher, and we got all the dust and debris which came out of the back of the thresher and we had to clear it up and it was an awful job to keep up with it. We harvested and then, of course, we ploughed and harrowed and then we planted, the full circle again. And we had to hoe the sugar beet in the summer, thin it out, and in the winter we harvested them, knee deep in mud and water, the tractor got them out and we had to go behind the tractor and chop the tops off. We had a few chopped hands.

Occasionally we had reapers and we did have some combine harvester that he [Hazel's husband, Bert] drove, that was a nice job, one driving the tractor, one sitting on the back of it, you turned the corn and sheaves and then you stood them up, and then threshed them afterwards, but the combine that was a machine. We girls went behind with tanks on trailers and when the combine was full, we'd run alongside and it was funnelled into our tanks, we had to take them back to an allocated place in the field and help fill the sacks. The only help we had to give was to get up in the tank and push the corn out through the hole. Well, at that time we had some Irishmen working and their great fun and delight was to put their fingers through the holes and when you got towards the bottom of the tank you had to use your feet to push the corn and – you can guess what happened – hands used to come through and pull your leg and you'd fall arse over head. It really was fun.

Working with Animals

Some jobs were more popular than others and many land girls seemed to enjoy working with animals. Peggy Pearce preferred animals to people. She worked with cows and pigs, and was particularly fond of pigs, something that her farmer commented on:

The sow had piglets and she used to be put out in the orchard, they have about six or seven, and they were only about that size, they were absolutely gorgeous, you pick them up, they squeak like mad, mum looks around to see what's happening, they go up against a tree, they do exactly what mother does, so funny. My farmer used to say to me: 'Are you going to do any work today, or are you going to lean over that fence watching the pigs?' But we got on well.

Peggy was moved to many different farms during her time in the Land Army, doing a variety of jobs, including working with horses:

Threshing in those days. You had to stook the corn up. I had to do the horse myself, I was only shown once, a great carthorse, I was shown once how to put the reins on, only once and you had to put the collar on and, of course, those Suffolk Punches are damn tall and I had to get the collar, tremendous weight, and as I went to put it over her head, she'd toss her head; it was a scream. I worked too hard really. We cut the hay by hand, this swathe, it was only iron, and you got up on the step, only a little seat, nothing to hold onto, and then I had to go along, get off the seat, push your foot down, turn the horse round, it turned the hay, then you did it another time.

We had to get the cows in at 6 a.m., then we were out in the fields until 10 o'clock when there was double summer time, not always but to get the harvest in.

(Peggy Pearce)

To this day, Peggy has great respect for most farm animals, apart from chickens.

Farming in the 1940s was still very primitive: land girls either cut down corn, thistles and other crops by hand, or used horse-drawn ploughs and carts. Beryl Peacham and her mother used a horse called Broughton to draw the milk cart. They had a small dairy in the farm house and had to roll the heavy churns through the hall and over a sandstone path before loading them onto the cart: 'You put your hand on the top of the lid and gripped it round, and you twisted the churn tight round with the other hand.' The horse was also used to pull the hay rake, a wide machine about 6 feet wide that was used to rake up hay: 'You used to hold the reins with one hand and pull the handle and press the thing at the same time. It was interlocked, so your foot helped your hand and that made piles come out of the back and sometimes you had to do it in rows about 15 feet long.' Much of the work was done by hand: 'we used to come along with our prongs and make it into haycocks. We had a wooden rake, with wooden tines, and you had to rake under the machine and keep drawing it out and moving it over gradually until you had a pile behind you. That was a hot job.' In the 1940s horses were essential to farming and it was a 'terrible day' for Beryl when the noise of Army manoeuvres frightened Broughton, an elderly hunter. He panicked, fell into a river and although Beryl managed to get him out, he died.

Rat Catching and Pest Control

One of the gutsier jobs was rat catching. Rural newspapers such as the *Sussex Express and County Herald* were full of advertisements featuring rats and urging their destruction, under the dramatic heading: 'Kill that Rat: It's doing Hitler's Work'. In the view of the authorities, the rat was second only to Hitler: the damage that could be done to the crops was enormous and war was waged on rodents, no less than the Nazis. For some land girls, such as Margaret Donaldson, the thought and reality of killing rats was quite repulsive:

I didn't do rat catching. There was one occasion when they harvest the hay, when they got to the middle, I didn't like this bit. All the farm workers used to stand around with their forks, ready to kill whatever was in there. I left it to the men. I was probably expected to do it, but I didn't.

Land girls were expected to kill rats and other pests if told to and many did, taking a pride in this achievement no less than in other areas of their work. In March 1942 the *Land Girl* included an account of gassing rats by L. Clarke, WLA member 58,547, a land girl in Leicester: 'Suddenly, out popped a brown head with two beady eyes. Bosh! One more of Hitler's helpers was removed, only a little helper...but one who can cause a deal of damage to our country's corn supply.' And in April 1944, the *Land Girl* magazine featured a picture of WLA member L. Roberts, 68196, from Flintshire and her dog who, between them, had killed 73 rats in 1 hour 40 minutes. Phyllis Cole regarded it as essential work: 'We used to have a bit of excitement because the rats used to come out as the stuff got to the bottom and then we'd all come round and have a bash. I had a go, I hate rats; they're vermin.'

Bulls, Bombs and Doodlebugs

Working on the land brought discomforts, mishaps and sometimes very real dangers. Countless land girls suffered severe exhaustion, weariness, aching backs, blistered feet and hands, chilblains, chapped fingers and lips, cuts, scratches, stings and bites. Many land girls experienced the pain of a heavy carthorse landing on their feet, or being knocked flying by a nervous cow; some, like Phyllis Cole, had the fearful experience of a charging bull running behind them and only her cool head and love of animals, kept her safe. The pages of the *Land Girl* and the *Land Army Manual* were packed with advice on how to look after wet clothing, how to put and take off gumboots more easily when feet were swollen (sprinkling a little French chalk inside them), how to remove bee stings, and many homemade remedies for cuts, bruises and chapped lips. There was also advice on how to lance blisters and how to harden soft hands and feet.

Accidents happened because of the nature of the work. It was quite common for land girls to chop off the tips of their fingers, if not their whole finger, when cutting the tops of sugar beets or other crops. Blanche Lucas suffered permanent damage to her hand:

We were cutting tops off swedes. We pulled the swedes – not particularly hard work but backbreaking. If you'd got a good back it didn't worry you. We pulled the swedes and had to scrape the dirt off and turn them over and chop the greenery off and I was chatting away to two or three others, not

First World War Women's Land Army

NOT the least of the discomforts which beset the "farmer's girl" are the chapped hands and roughened skin which result from the exposure to all weathers. In these cases Royal Vinolia Cream gives instant relief. Used regularly night and morning it keeps the complexion soft and clear, the hands free from redness and roughness. When the skin is broken by chaps, scratches or abrasions, the medicated and antiseptic properties of Vinolia Cream quickly soothe and heal the skin.

...dvert for Royal Vinolia Cream targeted ...pping caused by farm work. One of ...eral produced c.1916 aimed at land girls.

2. Advert for Royal Vinolia Talcum Powder for the farmer's girl who still wants soft skin as she ploughs the land for the war effort.

3. First World War land girls process through the street, ...ssibly as part of a recruitment drive.

4. Land girl ploughing during the First World War, an image that was used for advertisements in *The Landswoman* and other journals.

5. Land girls working with POWs.

6. Whilst some land girls such as Joan Markby were forced to live in huts with poor facilities, other were far luckier. Sheelah Cruttenden was billeted in Dumbleton Hall, the 'hostel'. Following a pre war visit by Nazi Ambassador Baron von Ribbentrop, Hitler had apparently decided to live at the hall had he succeeded in invading Britain.

THE LANDGIRL

Volume 4   AUGUST, 1943   Price 3d.

e bovine banner from *The Land Girl* magazine.

Land girl Joan Markby (née Moody)
...ing with cows on the farm. Initially, Joan
...een 'frightened of cows, terrified, I
...dn't go near them.'

10. Studio portrait of land girl Eileen Styles in her WLA uniform.

11. The official release card given to members of the WLA, thanking them for their services and recording their time in service. Eileen Styles was enrolled in the WLA from 1943–47, leaving two years after the war had ended.

WOMEN'S LAND ARMY (ENGLAND & WALES).

RELEASE CERTIFICATE.

The Women's Land Army for England and Wales acknowledges with appreciation the services given by

Miss E. A. Styles, W.L.A. No. 122990,

who has been an enrolled member for the period from

June, 1943 to 22nd November 1947

and has this day been granted a willing release.

Date 15.11.47.

WOMEN'S LAND ARMY.

By this personal message I wish to express to you

Miss E. A. Styles, W.L.A.No. 122990,

my appreciation of your loyal and devoted service

as a member of the Women's Land Army from

June 1943   to   November, 1947.

Your unsparing efforts at a time when the victory

of our cause depended on the utmost use of the

resources of our land have earned for you the

country's gratitude.

Elizabeth R

royal word of thanks from Queen Elizabeth, wife of George VI, for land girl Eileen Styles (later n Grabham).

13. Hazel Bannister (later King) was about 18 or 19 when she learned to drive a tractor; she received this certificate officially authorising her to drive any motor vehicle, including a tractor.

EAST SUSSEX COUNTY WAR AGRICULTURAL EXECUTIVE COMMITTEE

County Hall,
LEWES.

THIS IS TO CERTIFY that

Miss ...BANNISTER. H.
Mrs.

employed by this Committee is authorised to drive and use any vehicle, being the property of this Committee, in the group defined in his/her driving license under the Motor Vehicle (Driving Licenses) Regulations 1937.

Signed:............................

Executive Officer.

Signature of Driver H. Bannister

14. Hazel and her co-worker Marge on a tractor, ready to plough up Romney Marsh, Kent. 'Tractors were very basic then [but] I loved ploughing'.

-16. The award-winning land girl, Peggy Pearce (middle), the photo was also printed in *The Land*
l magazine which celebrated all of the WLA's achievements.

THE WOMEN'S LAND ARMY, SURREY.

SECOND **PRIZE**

Awarded to

Peggy Pearce.

in the

BEAUTY **Competition**

held at The Philanthropic School, Redhill,
2nd June, 1945.

18. Former land girl Denny working on a haystack, carefully balanced on a ladder.

19. Land girls leaning on a fence after a wedding: note the jaunty hat angles.

20. Hazel King (née Bannister), land girls, mechanic and the foreman, plus a 'hostel boy', one of boys from London who stayed in hostels and helped out on the land.

Farms needed year-round labour, no matter what the weather. Hazel King (née Bannister) and er land girls in the snow.

Land Army wedding: Hazel was in the guard of honour. The wedding took place in East lldeford church, 'we used pitchforks to make an arch'.

23. Land girl Peggy Pearce worked with a variety of animals on the dairy and mixed farms she worked for in the Bristol area and Surrey. Here, she's turning hay using horse-drawn machinery known as a turner.

24. Peggy and a friend with the big cart horse she was usually expected to handle alone, despite having only been shown how to do so once.

A group of land girls and a man – the 'threshing' gang take a break from harvesting the land.

Land girl Joan Markby (née Moody) and friend working with pigs at a time when meat was ̖rce nationwide. Joan was sleeping in a hut at the time and baths were rare events as the facilities ̖re so limited.

27. Betty Hamer (née Towse) in her full Land Army uniform.

28. Hazel King (née Bannister), who joined the WLA aged around 18, is seen here in her full Land Army uniform.

Peggy Pearce and a fellow farm hand in working clothes, believed to be for working in the dairy.

Peggy posing with fellow land girls in their uniforms.

31. The model land girl, a portrait shot taken of Cynthia, a friend of Eileen Styles, in Herne Bay, 1943.

Portrait shot of Joan Markby (née Moody) in her full Land Army uniform.

33. Eileen Hodd and her first husband, George, in the back garden. George was killed in a farming accident only three months after they married. 'I don't often talk about it, but it's all in the life of the Land Army.'

34. Eileen Hood (née Jarman) 'hop training', sitting on what was known as a 'hill'. The house in the background is where she lived with her family.

35. Eileen being lifted into the air by her friend Margaret surrounded by hops. In the summer, land girls often rolled up their trousers to make shorts. WLA officials were not always happy about this casual dress style.

37. Peggy Pearce (Land Army 1939–45) and friend stooking, or raking hay.

38. The Sussex WLA helped to raise money for the WLA Benevolent Fund by socials, such as this WLA Exhibition in Brighton, 1947.

Sussex Women's Land Army Exhibition
(In aid of the W.L.A. Benevolent Fund)

CORN EXCHANGE & PAVILION THEATRE, BRIGHTON

Monday, 17th February to Saturday, February 22nd

AGRICULTURAL EXHIBITS	M.O.I. FILMS DAILY
HANDICRAFTS	STALLS	SIDESHOWS
TRADE SHOWS	FORTUNE TELLER	MUSIC
	TEA GARDEN	ICES

ADMISSION 1/- (Children half price)   W.L.A. in Uniform 6d.
OPEN DAILY 2.30 to 8 p.m.

The W.L.A. Entertains
in
THE PAVILION THEATRE . . Nightly at 7 p.m.

MONDAY
Music and Mime

TUESDAY
W.L.A. Competitions

WEDNESDAY
B.B.C. Ensemble

THURSDAY
Brains Trust

FRIDAY
" Motive for Murder " (Play)

SATURDAY
Distribution of Prizes & Prize Winners' Concert
Contributions towards the Prize Money would be gratefully received

FRIDAY · DANCE · ROYAL PAVILION

For full details and where to book seats see following pages or posters
3

39. Sheelah Cruttenden, third row left, took part in this one-day strike in Cheltenham in April 1945. Some 150 WLA members were protesting against the Government's decision not to allow land girls post-war grants or training, unlike women in the Civil Defence or ATS. Striking land girls adopted the slogan, 'Give us a square deal, and we'll give you a square meal'.

ON A ONE-DAY STRIKE.—Some of the Women's Land Army girls in North Gloucestershire who came into
...ham on Friday, when they called a one-day strike as a protest against the non-granting of gratuities by
Government. These ...ere from hostels at Southam, Dumbleton Hall, Tetbury, and Oaklands.

. An advert placed after war ended both appreciating the work performed by the WLA and calling for their continued assistance on the land.

THE LAND GIRL

CHRISTMAS PARTY

robably the most vivid impression of special Six-year Christmas Party was he most surprising fusion (or mixture) stately ceremony, spontaneous gaiety constant movement. First, the 750 girls collected for the great march— how well they marched, under their arate banners, even those who were too ochind it to hear the fine band of His esty's Grenadier Guards, which led the way. Crowds cheered them all along the route, and a distinguished audience gave them a special ovation from the steps of St. Paul's, as they passed on their way to the Guildhall. Here, sitting on the floor, munching their sandwiches, they made an unusual gathering under the high, beautifully carved roof in this famous building. During lunch, Mrs. Jenkins gave informal but wonderfully clear instructions for the

January, 1946

41. This page from *The Land Girl* magazine shows 750 land girls marching through London as part of a special Christmas party to celebrate six years of the Land Army. When war ended in 1945, some 54,000 women were still working on the land; many continued until the WLA was disbanded in 1950.

42. When possible, the WLA organised social events for land girls, including dances such as this one in Brighton. Money raised from the dance was used to swell the coffers of the WLA Benevolent Fund which supported land girls who needed help with maternity and other health costs as well as help with retraining.

looking where my chopper was going and, yes, I cut the tendons over the knuckle; never been the same since and, of course, no compensation. I think I could have got compensation because we were insured but it didn't worry me. I didn't follow it up, so that was that.

The *Land Army Manual* strongly advised wearing gloves but many land girls ignored the advice; they found it was quite useless wearing gloves, which offered little or no protection and often made it difficult to carry out tasks. Beryl Peacham's extensive tasks, which included milking, feeding, cooling and delivering milk, mucking out, cleaning and cutting the hay, also included cutting hedges, which meant working:

> ...with a hand bill because we hadn't got any chainsaws. I didn't think it was too hard because I'd got quite strong arms but we didn't have such good gloves, so you got pricks, not just brambles but also blackthorn; their long thorns are lethal.

Newly trained tractor drivers were only too aware that if they approached the starting handle incorrectly, it could kick back and remove a thumb or hand. Threshing machines were dangerous too and more than one land girl knew someone who had lost an arm in the machine. Joan Markby and some of the other land girls were sometimes at one of the WLA organizer's houses where 'there was a Land Army girl there who had lost her arm in a thresher'. Taken all together, the idyllic looking farming life shown in the recruitment posters was far from accurate.

It was not only the work itself that brought dangers. Britain was

> I was in the fields with another girl and a doodlebug came by, so I pushed her flat to the ground and lay down myself; it was terrible. I think that was the worst time really. We were out in the country. We had our gas mask and that was it.
>
> (Berenice Birch, land girl, Kent)

at war and many land girls, particularly those working in the south of England were literally on the front line, or the flight path, as German bombers flew over Britain dropping their load on the way to or from London. From 1944, there were doodle-bugs as well. Hazel King, driving tractors on the exposed stretches of Romney Marsh, remembered various occasions when she had to dive for cover:

> We had the hit and run raids, you couldn't hear much on a tractor and if you knew there was something on, you got off your tractor and flew to the ditch, if there was a ditch handy, to get in it. By that time we'd been given tin hats and then, of course, [there was] the doodlebug. We had quite a few near misses. When I was working with Mavis, we'd got one girl driving the tractor and one girl sitting on the wing of the tractor, acting as a look out. We heard the doodlebug cut out and 'What do you do now?' we thought. So we saw it coming, we thought we'd run towards it, perhaps we could go under it, silly things you think, and we knew that further along in the hedge there was a gate and we could get through the gate into the next field and down behind the hedge, and we got in the next field but I don't remember getting in the field because we were blown over; by then it had come down and we think the explosion had knocked us over. It was quite frightening at times, but we didn't seem to care at that age. The war was on and that was that. It was a bit scary but I don't remember being petrified. The only near miss we ever had was [when we] were making a road, filling in the potholes in the road with rubble, and a doodlebug came over and we all got under the trailers and when it came down, I got up to have a look, didn't I? The next thing I knew the farmer hit me on the head with a shovel, and the doodlebug came down and in the next field these land girls struggled out of the ditch all covered in grass and one of them was crying but they were all right.

The *Land Girl* magazine and many others praised the courage of land girls who not only continued their work while the bombing raids were on but also, in many cases, used their initiative to put fires out and rescue both animals and humans. Land girls them-selves quite often played down the situation. In August 1940, the *Land Girl* included a letter from two volunteers in Essex – the magazine had a monthly section on news from the counties – who said:

> We are getting along splendidly. The air raids are horrid, but we just keep smiling. This is a very lonely and nasty place at times but we are not complaining...We are on the land now, doing all sorts of interesting jobs. We have done docking, sugar-beet singling...and are now thistle dodging.

Three months later, in November 1940, the *Land Girl* ran an article specifically about 'Land Girls under fire', referring to Dorset 'girls' being bombed at home and at work and, likewise, Kent volunteers, over 200 of whom were 'working on steadily in constant danger'. The East Kent secretary had been bombed out twice, and in East Sussex a land girl was the first on the scene to rescue two small children after a bombing raid.

Beryl Peacham, living and working in the South East, acted speedily when the farmhouse was bombed in the middle of the night:

> We always used to take our gumboots up to bed, and we had some border dogs. I took them into the shed; Mum went outside. Dad had left a whole row of buckets of sand. Mum took a couple and one bomb was literally one yard outside the kitchen window and it was just a miracle that it didn't fall on the roof, and then when I'd taken the dogs out and I knew Mum had gone in the orchard, I went around to see if the buildings were all right and I took buckets of sand as well but I soon ran out and wondered what the dickens could I use. Out in the cowshed we had some very sloppy manure that came out of the channels, so I went and got another smaller bucket and dipped it in and went around and put it down because Jerry was mooning around and one bomb had fallen next to a wooden wheel and that was on fire and I thought I'd better put that out first. Well, there were dozens. Maybe they just had this lot of incendiary bombs; they used to follow the railway line through Wadhurst and Etchingham and there was quite a lot of light, so they diverted and saw a big place like ours, with quite a lot of

buildings, and they must just have picked on it. The next day I took a couple of Hessian sacks and I filled each one; each bomb had a fin and I picked up 43 fins. The air raid warden came along the next day and said, 'You should have told me they were there'. We blooming didn't have time. Later on all the people were asked to go and watch a demonstration of how to put an incendiary bomb out – with a bucket of water and a stirrup pump. If I'd done that I wouldn't have got half of them done.

> There were [bombs] near the villages of the area and a German plane crashed just at the back of the farm building. They [doodlebugs] were horrible...we were really in a direct path to London. They used to cut out and then they would drop. I think there was a map somewhere of how many dropped from the coast and, of course, the planes used to come and shoot them down. We didn't have any [protective clothing], I never knew of any land girls around the area that had tin hats.
>
> (Eileen Hodd)

Long Hours and Low Pay

Few of the women interviewed for this book could remember exactly what they were paid during the war but it was very little. Not many were better off than they had been previously apart, perhaps, from those in domestic service. Most land girls took a drop in earnings when they joined the Land Army and throughout the war they were among the worst paid of women workers. Agricultural wages were low anyway; when war broke out male agricultural workers received an average weekly wage of 38/-, far lower than most unskilled men, and land girls consistently earned about half of that.

Lady Denman fought constantly to improve wages and conditions for land girls but, with such a scattered workforce, it was difficult to achieve consistency and the problem was compounded by the fact that farmers, although paid by the Government, employed and paid land girls. When war started, and after quite some battle with the Agricultural Wages Board, Lady Denman won a basic minimum wage for land girls of 28/-

a week for those over 18, which she considered the lowest wage on which volunteers could 'make do'. It was obviously far less than the male wage but the likelihood of land girls ever receiving equal pay with men was never really on the cards, and there were some WLA officials, including Vita Sackville-West herself, who did not really believe women were worth the same money as men.

As the war went on, Lady Denman managed to achieve better conditions. In 1940 the *Land Girl* announced that for the very first time a national minimum wage had been achieved for men working in agriculture, namely 48/- a week, and at the same time announced that, 'There is no national minimum for women, but every County Agricultural Wages Committee has fixed a new county minimum for women either at an hourly or a weekly rate'. This was an achievement and meant that although county wages for land girls varied, no farmer who employed a land girl could, by law, pay her less than the county minimum.

By March 1941 land girls' wages had risen to 32/- a week for all land girls aged 18 who were billeted off farms, and free board and lodging for land girls billeted on farms, with a wage of 16/- both based on a 48-hour working week, and an overtime rate of 8d an hour. In some counties, the rate was higher. By 1942 the rate had gone up to 38/- a week and by 1944, it had reached around 48/- a week for those billeted off farms. In practice, after money was taken out for board and lodgings, this meant that land girls were not left with much money for themselves. National Insurance and Unemployment Insurance were also deducted. Despite the pay rises, their wages remained pitifully low and far lower than their sisters in the Forces, who also received other benefits such as free soap and sanitary towels that land girls had to pay for.

Strictly speaking the working week was set at 48 hours in winter, and 52 in summer but, in practice, land girls worked far longer days, particularly during double summer time, when most worked until late in the evening. Eileen Hodd worked in mixed farming:

...corn and hay, hops, fruit, cows, sheep. You had to get to work at 7 o'clock and whatever the season was that's what you did. If it was haymaking, you were out collecting hay in the fields and loading it up. If it was fruit time, you were picking fruit, we had blackcurrants and raspberries and apple orchards. In the wintertime, you were probably sorting apples or taking cuttings from the fruit bushes and burying them; come the spring, you would lift them and sort out the best shoots and they would be re-planted in other fields. You finished at 5, you had a break at mid-day for your lunch. During the seasonal time with hay making and gathering in the corn, you worked in the evening because if it was fine weather, you had to get the job done, so you could be working until 9 o'clock. We only had Saturday afternoons and Sunday off. We worked Saturday mornings, until 12 o'clock and if it was seasonal work that had to be done, you worked Saturdays as well.

Some land girls worked on Sundays and even on Christmas Day: when it came to milking for instance, there were then, and are now, no free days. Land girls could claim overtime pay but holidays were rare and did not come with pay until 1944 when Lady Denman achieved a major success – not just for land girls, but also all agricultural workers – when she gained their right to one week's statutory holiday a year, with pay. Land girls who were injured could claim compensation although many did not, and were also entitled to free medical care, provided they had a medical card and had signed on with an approved panel doctor.

On their side, land girls had to agree to certain conditions, which were listed on their membership cards, notably: to be prepared to go wherever they were needed and not to leave the Land Army, without official approval. They were also expected to carry out their work in the 'good and cheerful way for which the Land Army has now rightly become famed'.

Plodding and Endurance

Despite all the hard work, the dangers, the long hours and low pay of working on the land, accounts from numerous land girls stress how much they enjoyed their work and how proud they were to be in the Land Army. At times, as Blanche Lucas said, their life could best be described as 'plodding and endurance, because we did plod and we did endure' but at other times, there was a real excitement and pride in the work. As one letter writer to the *Land Girl* magazine expressed it in 1943:

I have been asked a good many times lately what I think of the Women's Land Army...I have been in this Service since February 1941 and claim to know quite a bit about it now. I do not know much about the other Women's Services but I don't think any of them can beat ours...Of course things have not always been smooth. My first attempt to milk was doomed to failure. I had only just sat down on my stool, when I suddenly found myself travelling through space...I was told to water horses, and rode one of them straight into the pit...I can now do anything with horses and cattle...I have even given injections to horses. I can plough, row and harrow...I can use a scythe...I love my work and would not change it for any other...I am proud to be a member of the W.L.A.

(P. Holmes WLA 38126, the *Land Girl*)

Chapter 6

The Lumber Jills

I'm a gel wot measures timber in a saw mill,
I'm a timber-measurer-up, a lumber-jill...
(Vera Lloyd, quoted in Meet the Members)

NOT ALL land girls worked in farming; some were employed in forestry as timber workers, measuring, felling, and managing trees. Nicknamed 'timber jills', 'lumber jills' or even 'polecats', they cut and hauled timber, toppled trees, cut poles for mineshafts, loaded charcoal and made wooden roads. They handled horses, billhooks and a whole range of saws and lived in huts, billets or camps sometimes deep in the forests of England, Wales and Scotland, often far from other workers and frequently in very basic conditions.

The Women's Timber Corps

Forestry was even less of a woman's world than farming. Before the war fewer than 200 women were employed in timber production and then only for light work in forests and saw mills. Men did the really heavy work of forestry: felling, sawing and hauling. Britain imported most of its timber products such as telegraph poles and pit props but with the coming of war the need to increase home-produced wood for pit props, railway sleepers, telegraph poles, wooden runners for tanks and even coffins became desperate. As male workers were called up, women were needed to replace them, and the obvious place to find them was through the Women's Land Army.

The WLA made its first appeal for women forestry workers in

1940, following the German occupation of France, when Britain expected to be invaded and it was realized there was an urgent need for wood to make barricades. Many women responded to the appeal and within a fairly short time nearly 1,000 land girls were doing forestry work in England and Wales. By 1942, however, not only had the demand for timber and timber workers increased dramatically – timber imports were being badly hit by submarine attacks on Allied shipping – but it was also felt that a specially trained expert unit was required for the work so with that in mind an offshoot of the WLA was set up in March 1942, which was known as the Women's Timber Corps. Two months later the *Land Girl* magazine announced to its readers that:

…A Women's Timber Corps has now been formed as a section of the Women's Land Army. New recruits who want to become timber workers are sent for four weeks training to a timber camp, where they learn to use the saw, the bill-hook and the axe, to lop, to chop, to fell and to handle timber. If at the end of training they are accepted for membership of the Timber Corps, they are seconded for service for the duration of the war with the Home Timber Production Department of the Ministry of Supply, which takes over from the Land Army full responsibility for their placing, billeting and welfare. The Timber Corps will…have a special badge and distinctive headgear. Then no Land Army procession will be complete without its contingent of green berets!

A Specialist Branch

As the *Land Girl* described, the Women's Timber Corps was effectively a sub-section of the Land Army. Women were recruited and enrolled through the WLA and Lady Denman was the honorary director. Volunteers were sent for training to one of the various camps established by the Home Timber Production Department of the Ministry of Supply, which might be in Suffolk or Wales. If the trained recruit was then considered suitable for the work, she was registered as a member of the Timber Corps and either employed by the Ministry of Supply or by a timber merchant working for the Ministry. From this point the Land Army itself had little to do with the timber workers: instead the Ministry was responsible for supervising the women and for their welfare, members of the Timber Corps being effectively seconded for the duration of the war.

From the beginning, forestry work was seen as a specialist area of work and one that required particular expertise. The work was only offered to those considered suitable and required higher qualifications than usual than other recruits into the Land Army. Members also received a higher starting wage of 45/- a week. Hardly surprisingly land girls were often suspicious of

The Uniform of the Women's Timber Corps

- 2 green jerseys
- 2 pairs of riding breeches
- 2 overall coats
- 2 pairs of dungarees
- 6 pairs of woollen knee socks
- 3 beige knit shirts
- 1 pair of boots
- 1 pair of brown shoes
- 1 pair of gumboots or boots with leggings
- 1 green beret
- 1 melton overcoat
- 1 oilskin or mackintosh
- 2 towels
- 1 green armlet and a metal badge, and Bakelite hat badge

their higher paid sisters, and lumber jills themselves often considered they were members of a rather elite work force. One member reflecting back on her time in the Timber Corps commented: 'We Timber Girls were snooty. We thought that we were better than the Land Girls because we worked harder and we got more pay.'

Outwardly, there was little to tell them apart. Lumber jills wore much the same uniform as the land girls, with one striking difference: a rather rakish green beret, as opposed to the brown slouch hat. Their badge reflected their occupation: it showed a fir tree surmounted by a crown, as opposed to the wheat sheaf badge of the land girls. The public then, and even now, knew even less about the Women's Timber Corps and the work of its members than they did about the land girls, and timber workers consider that they received even less recognition. It was not until October 2007 that the first British memorial to their work was erected, in Aberfoyle, Scotland.

Training Recruits

The original 1,000 land girls, who had already been working in forestry, were by now seasoned and experienced workers and formed the nucleus of the new Corps. Other volunteers rushed to join them. The Timber Corps was a popular destination: at one point women were volunteering at a rate of 250 per month. By the end of the first year the Corps' strength had risen to nearly 5,000 women, of whom 3,900 were working in England and Wales, and about 1,000 in Scotland; eventually, some 6,000 women served in the Timber Corps, 4,000 of them in England and Wales and 2,000 in Scotland. In July 1943 recruitment ended because the authorities wanted to direct women into other, less popular, areas of war work.

Recruits came from a wide range of backgrounds and jobs; they included hairdressers, private secretaries, shop assistants, librarians, musicians and at least one former ballet dancer. All were sent on four weeks' training courses. In Scotland, where the priority was to fell and prepare pit props, the emphasis was on training women for general forestry work, although they were also given the opportunity to learn how to work in sawmills and in haulage work with tractors and horses. In England and Wales, demand was more varied. Training might take place in a training camp in the middle of a forest, or a private country house that had been commandeered for the war. Conditions were often very basic and women soon learned to rough it. One training centre in Scotland was based at Shandford Lodge in Angus, a shooting lodge. Trainees lived in army huts, slept on army cots under rough grey blankets and used outdoor toilets.

One timber worker, Annice Gibbs, was sent to Chippenham in Wiltshire, for training:

> We camped in Nissan huts – 12 women in a hut. The floors were rough concrete and in the centre was a slow combustion boiler which did not give out much heat. Each bed was

made of slat wood...and covered with only a thin biscuit palliasse for a mattress. It was cold and dreary. On our first day in the woods, wearing thick, heavy boots, gaiters and dungarees, we lifted the heavy pit-props on to a trailer. The women came from all walks of life and this heavy work was foreign to them. Needless to say the beds did not exactly soothe our aching bones...
(quoted in *Women at War*, Carol Harris, Sutton Publishing)

During the first week trainees covered fairly general work, and were introduced to some of the main aspects of forestry work such as felling, cross-cutting, clearing woods, sawing, measuring, tractor and lorry driving. Over the next three weeks, training focused on more specialist areas, depending on the work women were going on to do. Experienced male foresters were used to train the new recruit.

Pat Parker joined the Timber Corps when she was 18. She went into a Land Army office in London and asked to join:

I'd recently seen an article in the *Daily Sketch* about the Timber Corps, women working in the woods. And I thought that was a job that would suit me. I was at the age when I was reading romances and my mind was full of pictures of strong men, hunky lumberjacks!

She was told that she would not be able to go home for six months but, nothing daunted, she decided that she would join up and, in due course, was sent to training at Culford. She left from Fenchurch Station, where there were a group of other young women, also on their way to Culford:

The train came in – I think Mum was worried, but she didn't show it...I sat down and thought again, 'oh God, what have I done?' But the girls were talkative and we all told each other what we did. One was a hairdresser. There was a secretary, a salesgirl...and Lil, sitting opposite me. She had been humping sacks of coffee around in a warehouse...At Culford we were taken by lorry to the camp, and we were there for a month. We were taught how to sharpen and use a saw and an axe, how to tell one piece of wood from another, one tree from another. And

I can still remember all of that...the fun part was learning to chop a tree down. First we were given stumps...We laughed about that because they were only about four feet high. One of the male instructors gave us each an axe and told us to have a go. Being daft and not knowing, we chipped away as though we were chipping matchsticks. We hadn't a clue. The instructor came back laughing and said, 'No, that's not the way. Let me show you.' Down swished the axe, then another chop and he cut a lovely V-shape in the tree. A couple of the girls swung the axe, missed the trunk and the weight of the axe swung them round full circle. We laughed so much in that first week, and our muscles ached...

('The Rewards of Hard Labour', Pat Parker, from *What Did You Do in the War, Mummy?*, Chatto & Windus).

Pat went on to learn criss-cross sawing, using a long saw with handles on both ends, a woman at each end, and was then taken into the forests to cut her first tree:

When the tree was ready to fall, we yelled 'Timberrrrr' and with a crack and a whoosh, down it came. We cheered. We'd done it. We were always very tired. But as we were such great pals together it hardly bothered us. We were a group of about fifty girls in the camp, and there were about ten or fifteen of us in the huts. (Pat Parker op. cit.)

When the month's training was over, qualified recruits were formally enrolled in the Timber Corps and then sent to their working destinations, which were usually far from home.

Types of Work

Vita Sackville-West commented that 'the Timber Corps girl has done an astonishingly good piece of work' and she was absolutely right. Lumber jills did a enormous range of forestry jobs: labouring in the forests; working in sawmills; acquisition work – going around the country deciding which trees should be, in Vita Sackville-West's words, 'sacrificed to the country's needs' but, more prosaically, checking how much was available for war production; pole-selection, which meant finding trees that could be selected for use as such things as telegraph poles or barricades, and measuring. Timber women carried out censuses of trees, negotiated with farmers and landowners to purchase trees on behalf of the ministry, did paperwork, keeping meticulous records, and worked with a range of unfamiliar tools and equipment including axes, cross-saws, billhooks, levers, wedges, cant hooks and the other tools of the forestry trade. Not only did they fell trees, and cut timbers to size, they also learned to haul and transport wood, working with heavy horses, tractors and even rafts, in all weathers and under all conditions.

Many of the men who had spent all their lives among the trees were called into the Army. Girls took over the woods, swung axes, drove tractors and loaded lorries. For the men in the front lines must have guns, and guns need coal, and to mine this coal we must have pit props. And because we must save ships and shipping space, the props have to come from our own forests.

(Della Smith, Timber worker, *Meet the Members*)

The work was absolutely essential for the war effort and members of the Timber Corps, many of whom had no previous experience, quickly learned to adapt to the strenuous work, and potentially dangerous tasks. They worked with men, including Canadian foresters who were, in the main, extremely helpful. Some foremen, however, were far less so. When Pat Parker finished her training, she asked to be sent with her friend Lil to Cornwall but:

...typical Army, we got sent in the opposite direction – up Hereford way. We became general foresters: you name it, we did it. The measurers were the brains of the outfit. They did the paperwork. They'd find a wood, talk to the farmer and sort out how much it would cost, make the arrangements to get the timber out, and do all the measuring. They'd mark the trunks that would have to come down...

We had to work for a male foreman, and on the first day he said, 'Right, you two, see those logs there, well put them over behind that there stick'. He just left us to it. You felt with a lot of the men you had to do twice as much to prove a point. You had to be a cussed sort of person – which I am...I had no muscles at all...but I eventually got myself fit, helped by Lil...She'd heave and I'd push until I got strong enough to heave, too...

Lil and I on our bikes – which were supplied to us at a cost of one shilling per week – always got up to the woods early. We'd have a fire going for the girls when they arrived from the hostel. In the thick of work it was bitterly cold. We'd leave the house wearing our big coats and as many jumpers as we could pile on. Then we'd do a bit of sawing and the coat would come off, and we'd be down to our shirt sleeves...I helped pull the timber out from the tree. I helped in the sawing and the loading of the timber, from four-foot-six-props, the first I ever loaded, to six-foot-six ones that went across the lorry. Then I graduated to nine-foot-pit props, the heavy ones.

Our driver and his mate made up the loading crew: two on the ground and two on the lorry to stack. To load logs two poles were placed from the ground to the lorry bed. The logs were then rolled up the poles and stacked. Once the bed was full, we raised the poles higher on to the stack and this process was repeated until we had four or five layers, the last layer being the hardest. We then drove to the railway station, and unloaded them into coal trucks. Two, sometimes three loads a day...

One of the filthiest jobs was stacking sacks of charcoal onto lorries. The dust from the charcoal choked the women and penetrated through layers of clothing to the skin, making the workers black all over. It was difficult for the women to get clean again, particularly given the wartime water restrictions. Pat did charcoal stacking, which she described as a 'filthy, rotten job' and also made roads:

There was a slope up into the woods and in the winter, when the rains came with lorries going up and down, it would turn into a quagmire...The boss said we must get a road built before the bad weather really hit us. So we went to a sawmill and picked up slats of wood...and laid these all the way up. Then we chucked tons of sawdust over it, so that it would eventually work down into the ground...

Walking for Miles

Before any timber products could be made, trees had to be selected, acquired from landowners, measured, marked with paint and recorded on a census, so that foresters coming behind could access the trees that were needed. Members of the Timber Corps who did this work walked for literally miles every day, and could be transferred at a moment's notice to forests all over the country. In many cases, their job was made harder because road and other signs had been removed for fear of enemy invasion.

One recruit to the Timber Corps, Anstace Goodhart, had expected that she would be planting trees but, on turning up to work with a mattock, a dibber and a spade, was informed that she was needed to help measure trees, not plant them. She started work in a large conifer forest, and:

> ...though I did not understand what we were doing at the time, I realise now that we were measuring up sample tenths of an acre. I soon became quite adept at pacing out a square chain and writing down the girths of trees as they were called out by the young man (an Assistant Acquisition Officer). The next afternoon I learned to distinguish between the various conifers in the wood...I was also promoted to girthing the trees, and I...remember the absurd pleasure I got from shouting out 'six and a quarter', 'seven and a half'...it really sounded as if I knew what I was doing...

Subsequently she went on to work with another woman, working in acquisitions and was broken in with a vengeance:

> We were told to go all through a colossal wood and measure and mark with white paint every oak tree over 14" quarter girth. The floor of the wood was one mass of brambles and briars, and often the only way to get to the tree was to crawl on one's hands and knees with the paintbrush between one's teeth. And when we eventually reached the tree it often

turned out to be 12½" or 13", and so the journey was useless. For two days we worked in this wood and, at last, completed it…

Then we were moved at a moment's notice to another village and a fresh billet…with only one bed and a lilo on a couch. I slept on the lilo to start with, but I had to be penned in with chairs and suitcases as I always fell out…We worked in a very nice wood opposite…and…were taught to measure the height and estimate the taper of individual trees. We scraped a piece of bark off each tree (which generally meant scraping a piece off one's knuckles too…) and then we painted a number on it and recorded the measurements…

For the next six months or so we had a very roving commission and only stayed a week or two at each place. It was a bitterly cold and snowy winter but only on two days did the weather make us cease fire (or should it be seek fire)…Several times we had rush jobs with a fixed time limit. In the winter it often meant working until it was too dark to see whether the tree had been marked or not…Some days everything went wrong; we tripped over with the paint, lost the paintbrush, lost our sense of direction and marked all the trees twice…experience…taught us always to have a spare pot of paint and brush…

…we were sent to my home county and told to make a census of all the pit wood still standing…The census was hard work, as often the woods were a long way from the road over ploughed fields, and we reckoned that had we carried a pedometer it would have recorded some ten to fifteen miles a day…

(quotes from *Meet the Members: A Record of the Timber Corps of the Women's Land Army*)

Pole selecting also involved walking for miles in order to find trees that were sufficiently straight for use as telegraph poles, pit props and barriers. According to one timber worker: 'We usually had to comb a wood backwards and forwards, in lines, looking for suitable trees.' In another account, which Vita Sackville-West reproduced in her book *The Women's Land Army*, a timber worker called D.E. Bellchamber described the difficulties of just getting to the job in wartime, particularly without public transport:

> We were quite a happy crowd...The food was the worst thing...the way it was cooked...The rice was so hard it was like chicken feed, the potatoes were cooked with dirt on them...we only had three sandwiches to last a full day in the woods...
>
> (Annice Gibbs, Timber Corps, *Meet the Members*)

Our next job was at Oare. We were to contact a foreman at Porlock where we had to put up for the night. We just got a last room at a hotel there...The next day we were up and out before we offended them...and as there was no bus until 4 p.m. we walked all the way. First we could not get to know the way...There were no signposts anywhere, and it was still raining. We got to Oare finally, and were told Brendon was five miles away.

Tellingly, her account of staying in the hotel spoke volumes about how some members of the more privileged classes regarded women timber workers and land girls with disdain. When Miss Bellchamber and her colleagues arrived at the hotel, they were asked if they wanted any dinner but, their funds being low, they opted for bread, cheese and tea. They chose to eat in the dining room but immediately realized they had made a mistake:

> ...the other guests were all in evening dress, and let us know how disgusting it was to let the Land Army into their hotel, and two left their dinner and went out, we could have eaten it we were so hungry. The next day we were up and out before we offended them again...

After doing various jobs in the woods in the district, she was sent to the New Forest:

> I did not know the New Forest was so big till we started to

walk through it. Twice we got lost, and my friends from home sent me a compass. We started trying to take short cuts and found ourselves miles from where we should have been…We had eight lodgings in different towns in the Forest and reckoned we walked 600 miles…It must be realised we are walking all the time we are working, and when you get into say 50-acre woods and have to explore from one end to the other, going up and down the lines of trees, once can soon cover a few miles…

It's funny, it's only in the last couple of years that people have begun to realise that the lumber jills existed. The Land Army didn't take to us during the war (and have more or less ignored us since). At the dance in the village hall, when they'd call out 'Land Army only. Step into the middle for a special Land Army Paul Jones', we'd join in at first. But we soon gave up, for they made it clear they didn't like it. I think it was because they had such lousy hours and we had an eight-to-five job. Yet our work was mucky, like theirs. We didn't have to get up at four to milk the cows…But we did just as hard a physical job…

(Pat Parker.)

Explaining to Others

Most people outside the Timber Corps, including land girls, had little or no idea of what the timber workers actually did, and there were many misconceptions. One pole-selector commented that her work was one of the jobs that 'the Land Army seem to know nothing about, judging from the interest my partner and I have excited on the rare occasions of our meeting them…We have never yet been successful in removing the rooted idea in people's minds that we actually climb trees to find out their height.'

To counteract some of these misconceptions, Vita Sackville-West, in her history of the WLA, gave quite detailed explanations of the job of the Timber Corps, including an article from *Woman* in which an unnamed lumber jill explained exactly what was involved in measuring trees:

Measuring involves the holding of a long tape along the length of the tree and the encircling of the central girth with another tape. In muddy weather, whichever of us does the girthing is unluckiest. If you ever try walking round a log which is coated with mud you will know what I mean; but if you go one step further and try to place a tape round its middle, I advise you to wear your oldest clothes. My 'other half' shares my daily life, and between us we cope with the office management of the mill and are responsible for the entire measuring of the incoming and outgoing timber. We share a small wooden hut in which we struggle with division, subtraction, and addition, brew weak tea and eat queer sandwiches. In the summer it is a grand life, but in the winter it is no good leaving your sense of humour behind...

Timber is one of the most vital munitions of war, but the manpower available was not sufficient to supply our minimum needs. In this emergency an appeal was made to women to help with home timber production. Many people would not believe that women could, or would, take the place of men. Experience...has triumphantly proved how wrong they were. All honour to the girls who, as volunteers, faced exile from home, the cold and mud of winter, long hours and heavy work, to do a job of first importance for their country.

(Sir Gerald Lenanton, Director, Home Timber)

Timber workers also wrote to the *Land Girl* describing their work and, in around 1945, some of their accounts together with poems were published in a small book called *Meet the Members: A Record of the Corps of the Women's Land Army*. Profits from the sale of the book (reprinted by the Imperial War Museum in 1997) were donated to the Women's Land Army Benevolent Fund.

One account from two timber workers concerned felling trees, one of the most skilled jobs in forestry. Their first attempt was not very satisfactory:

...we made our first attack on the standing trees. Our self confidence received a check at our first attempt. The manager came along and found four of us pushing at a tree and, when he asked us what we were doing, we said, 'Trying to push it down'. This amused him immensely, but he initiated us into the use of a sledge and wedge – and we never again wasted our strength…

The account then went on to describe, for the benefit of fellow members, what was actually involved in felling a tree, from making the first 'dip', a wedge-shaped cut close to the bottom of the tree, through to sawing the tree, cutting off the 'stubb shoot', trimming or cutting off the branches and the top of the tree, a procedure known as 'snedding' and having it ready for the hauliers to take to the mill.

Loving the Work
Women worked in sawmills as well as in the forest. Vita Sackville-West considered this particular area of work:

…a terrifying task, as anyone who has watched the great toothed circular saws whirring with murderous speed and sharpness will agree. It is a task which requires extreme care, precision, and concentration, for the saw which will travel with prolonged and undeviating ruthlessness up the solid trunk of wood will slice in one second through the soft finger…Men have been known to shake their heads and say no, it didn't take their fancy; but the girls of the Timber Corps have done it…

Sawing was without doubt a skilled and dangerous business but nevertheless members of the Women's Timber Corps replaced men in the sawmills too. Surprisingly, there were not many accidents. Descriptions in *Meet the Members* of timber workers who were employed in sawmills were extraordinarily blasé and made light of any of the difficulties encountered, although one woman, Muriel E. Wild, who worked in a sawmill in Suffolk for 18 months, mentioned that when she reported for work on the first day, the foreman greeted her with the comment that he had 'never wanted women working for me, but I suppose nothing can be done about it now'.

Members of the Timber Corps minded that they were not better known but most wrote of their pride in their work, and their love of being employed in the grandeur and wonder of forests. Many developed an abiding love of trees and the natural world around them that continued well after the war.

At Home and Abroad

Britain was not the only Allied country that had a WLA, nor women timber workers. As the war continued, Land Armies were formed elsewhere. In July 1942 the Australian Women's Land Army (AWLA) was formed as a national organization. Its aim, as with its British counterpart, was to replace male farm workers who had either signed up to fight or who were working in other essential war work. It was organized on similar lines to the British WLA, with membership open to women aged from 18 to 50 who were British subjects or immigrants from Allied nations. Women could either be fulltime members or auxiliary members, working for periods of not less than four weeks at designated times. Most recruits came from the cities and, like their counterparts in Britain, were initially regarded with scepticism by farmers. They were housed in hostels, trained and provided with uniforms. By 1942 Tasmania had recruited some 250 members. In October 1942 the *Land Girl* included greetings to the British WLA from Tasmania, and in particular from the 'Jennyroos', as the Tasmanian members called themselves – Jennyroo being the female version of Jackaroo, or apprentice farmer.

> As more young men have to be called to the Forces, the Women's Timber Corps must play a still bigger part in the production through the critical offensive year of 1944...the more timber you produce or help to produce, the more ships are released from the offensive. During 1942 some workers in the Women's Timber Corps were saving shipping space at the rate of 50 tons a year.
>
> (Home Timber Production Department, Ministry of Supply)

At its peak in December 1943, there were 2,382 permanent members and 1,039 auxiliary members, working an average week of 48 hours. In contrast to women in Britain, the Australian Minister for Labour recommended improving the status of the AWLA by making it an official fourth service, a decision that the

Australian Cabinet endorsed. In the event, arrangements were not completed until 1945, which is when the AWLA was disbanded, so Australian land girls did not receive the same benefits as women in the other services. Since 1997, former members have been eligible for the Civilian Service Medal.

New Zealand had its own WLA and the United States also recruited women to work on the land. By summer 1942 American farmers were facing a severe labour shortage, with some 6 million farm labourers having left the fields for wartime factory work or the armed services. Appeals went out through radio stations and newspapers for volunteers to replace them, and women responded. By 1943 a female corps had been formed, known as the Women's Land Army. Recruits did not have to have previous farming experience but did need to be 'physically fit, patriotic, curious and patient'. The American WLA recruited about 1 million women, from as varied backgrounds as their British colleagues: college students; beauticians, accountants, bank clerks, teachers and others. Here too, overseas links were made, particularly when First Lady Eleanor Roosevelt visited Britain in December 1942 and made a particular point of visiting the Land Army in Warwickshire.

Chapter 7

Living with Others

*U*nlike other women's war services, it is rare for members of the Land Army to work in groups. Most have to carry on their jobs without the comradeship of fellow members and often in lonely circumstances....
(Lady Denman, the *Land Girl*, April 1940)

WAR DISRUPTS normal living patterns and for most women joining the Land Army meant embarking on a completely new experience. It was not just the work that was new but also encountering people from varied backgrounds, often far from home and living in strange billets, on farms or in hostels. While some worked in gangs or lived boarding-school style in crowded hostels, many land girls worked and lived in isolation. And for those who came from towns and cities, it was like entering a new world.

Leaving Home

Many new recruits were leaving home for the first time. Homesickness was fairly common, although could be eased by encountering other young women in the same situation. One Londoner, Ellen Grabham, joined the Land Army in 1943 and was sent to Rye in Sussex:

> It wasn't too bad because there were 12 of us who all met on Charing Cross station and we went to Ashford and a coach met us at Ashford and we went on to Romney Marsh, but the food was horrible in the New Church Hostel. We had no tea to take with our lunch, we had to buy milk, we had a beer bottle and we used to fill it up with milk... [I wasn't

homesick] because I was with a lot of girls all my own age.

Helen Dawson was only billeted ten miles from her home, but had never been that far from home before:

It felt like a strange country. I used to bike home to see my mum, I was homesick. I had lost my father when I was 14 so I only had my mother and we were very close, like sisters.

Beryl Peacham, who worked on the farm where her parents were tenant farmers, did not have to deal with the trauma of leaving home but she remembers that other land girls were bitterly homesick:

The land girls who had been working in hairdressers, they found such a terrible change, they had never been outside Brighton, some of them. We had one girl with us, she came from Brighton and she was so homesick it was incredible; she was really terribly homesick. I tried to help her. I was showing her how to feed the cows and cut up the hay with the knife and those things that she had to learn. She had to learn milking but she couldn't get the hang of it and after a fortnight she asked to go.

Another young recruit from mid-Wales was sent to Kent and found the change from a lively family life difficult to cope with:

It was so quiet and lonely. I didn't like it. I'd got five brothers and a sister at home. I was homesick to start with. It was great when they sent me here [Brenzett hostel, Kent].

English land girls who were sent to Wales found the new culture equally strange, particularly when they were sent to Welsh-speaking areas.

Billets and Farms

Some land girls had the relative luxury of living at home, with mothers who cooked and washed for them. Others were sent to farms or forests far from home. They were placed in billets or lodgings, or lived on the farms where they worked. Some were billeted singly; others shared lodgings with one or more land girls. Living conditions varied enormously and could be very basic: many cottages and farms did not have running water, bathrooms or inside lavatories. The attitudes of farmers and landladies to the land girls billeted with them also varied. Some land girls were made welcome and treated well; others had bad experiences.

Peggy Pearce was sent to many different farms during the war. During her training, she was billeted in a 'beautiful mansion' where she shared a bedroom with another girl, that was right up in the loft. There was a big clock outside their window that chimed every half hour but she and her friend were young, and usually exhausted after the day's work, and they just slept through. After training she was sent to a farm outside Bristol. The farmer and his family were welcoming and treated her well. She was billeted in the village where her landlady:

> …was a very hard lady. She had two children. Oh, she was hard. The father was in the army. And the poor little boy [landlady's son], you know boys are difficult with food. If he didn't eat his lunch, or his dinner, it was given to him for his supper and if he didn't eat it then, it was given to him for his breakfast. So, I had a big bag and I put my hand out and I put it all in this bag and she said, 'There you are, I knew you'd eat it in the end'. And we had leeks, her husband grew leeks, and all that was left were the leeks. She wasn't a very good cook and I had to share a bed with her daughter. Luckily, he [the farmer] said to me one day 'Would you like to come and billet with us?' and I said 'Oh, golly yes'. I didn't tell him I wasn't happy. And then they asked my friend if she would like to come up; she wasn't at the farm, but anyway she came up and billeted with me. We slept in the same bed. [Lack of privacy] didn't bother me. I had a sister and we shared a bedroom.

In contrast to her billet, life on the farm was more comfortable: 'It was a beautiful farmhouse, three rooms, dining room, kitchen and she'd [farmer's wife] put this oil lamp on; both of us had lunch at the middle of the day, the main meal, she was a lovely cook. We lived on the fat of the land there.' The farmer's wife also did her washing.

Margaret Donaldson was billeted with the minister and his family at the Manse in Coddenham, East Suffolk and was well treated. Every morning the minister woke her at 4.30 and had already prepared a pot of tea. The family was kind and did everything for her including the cooking and her washing. Her room only contained a bed, cupboard, dressing table and, of course, a Bible, but by comparison with her own home, she thought it was the height of luxury:

> I had my own room and bed. I came from a big family so it was a great luxury. My mother had 10 children. When we were very young, there were about four of us in a bed. It was delightful to have my own room, wonderful, really special.

When she left the Manse, the family presented her with a Bible, inscribed with the words, 'Margaret, it has been wonderful to know you. Please read and search the scriptures.'

Phyllis Cole too had 'wonderful' digs with a 'lovely' landlord but she knew that not all land girls were as fortunate. She heard of land girls who were 'put up in a hall and they said it was cold, absolutely dreadful'.

Pamela McDowell worked on a small farm, surrounded by council houses, and was billeted in one of the houses. She had a tiny bedroom with a rag rug on a linoleum floor, a chest of drawers and an iron bed and found it extremely bleak. She was the only land girl employed on the farm and the farmer just assumed that she knew what she was doing and left her to get on with the work. She was probably too scared to admit that she could not manage. After about three months, her mother visited and was so appalled by the conditions that a transfer was arranged.

Water was rationed during wartime and hot water was limited. Baths, when they were available, could not be deeper than 4 or 5 inches and many land girls had to wash in cold water, which made it even harder to remove the accumulated filth caused by working on the land. Outdoor lavatories were common, which could be a shock to those used to more comfortable facilities.

Having started her first job on a farm in Dorset, Joan Markby requested a transfer and at her next posting ended up sleeping in a hut.

> I went off to Maiden Newton near Dorchester and that was really milking and cows and pigs. We slept in a hut. Sometimes there was just me and then my friend came who I had gone into the Land Army with, they got her there and then there was an Irish girl, who came later on and a girl from the village. And sometimes there were four of us in the hut and sometimes none. There wasn't any heating in the hut, it was very cold, there was a double bed and two singles in there, lack of privacy wasn't a problem, it was fun. We put pin-ups all over the wall, all the American generals and the film stars and all our friends, we covered the wall, they didn't mind because it was only a hut. We had a lovely time.

Amenities on the farm where Joan was working were basic, and washing was a problem:

> We couldn't do much washing, there wasn't any electricity on the farm, there was one stove in the kitchen, like an Aga, which we used to come to in the morning and warm our backsides on and that was for cooking and it also heated the water. Well, there were up to eight people on the farm, so water, hot water, was very limited for washing and clothes, so I used to take them home when I did go home to mum. We had to wash what we could, you can imagine with one load of water and [all] these people. If we got a bath it was wonderful.

When Peggy Pearce went to work on a farm at Englefield Green, Surrey, the farmer gave her a farm cottage to live in. She remembered that, 'I had my home in a cottage. You had to duck to go in [and] the toilet was in the garden. It was in the middle of the field and I had to walk to the farm.'

Another two land girls who shared a small cottage in

Lincolnshire had no running water, an outside dry privy, and washed in cold water using a bowl in the bedroom. A timber worker who was billeted in Cumbria, and had to share a bed with a co-worker found, to her horror, that there was no running water or electricity and that the two of them had to wash in about a pint of cold water. In her written account, Pat Parker of the Women's Timber Corps, described one house where she and her friend Lil were billeted:

> ...we slept in the same bed...There was no bathroom in the house so we'd go for a proper bath to the public baths – the swimming baths, I mean, for in those days they had hot baths on the sides. At home we'd get the hot water on and, as we used to say, wash up as far as possible and down as far as possible and leave possible to chance. We often washed our hair under the old pump in the back kitchen... ('The Rewards of Hard Labour', Pat Parker, quoted in *What Did you Do in the War, Mummy?* Chatto & Windus)

Grated Carrot Sandwiches

Food was as variable as the lodgings. Working long hours in the open air sharpened appetites and most land girls were constantly hungry. Land girls, unlike other women workers, were entitled to double rations, and they gave their ration books to the farmers and landladies to buy their food. Farmers' wives and landladies were supposed to provide breakfast and a cooked evening meal, and most land girls were given packed lunches, usually consisting of sandwiches and a flask of tea. Food was usually adequate, if basic, but sandwiches were often a source of irritation and annoyance. Hazel King was billeted in a hostel while she was training to be a tractor driver:

> We were all girls and we were well looked after, but mind you we had funny packed lunches. We had cheese and that sort of thing, but I do remember that at least once a week we had grated raw carrot sandwich, which we got used to and we ate it because we were always hungry. But what was horrible was cold baked beans sandwiches. Some threw

them away but I always ate mine, and then we had a cooked meal in the evening...

Beetroot was another common sandwich filling and almost universally disliked. There was the added disadvantage that if it rained, the dye ran out of the beetroot, turning a sandwich into a red, soggy mess. Many land girls were unable to face beetroot again once the war was over. Occasionally landladies cheated on ration books and held back food that should have been given to land girls. The authorities came down very heavily on a landlady who stored food for her own use.

Meals themselves were sometimes almost inedible and, in some cases, land girls were not allowed to eat with the family but were given their food separately. One land girl was billeted with a widowed farmer. His housekeeper took a strong dislike to her and refused to speak to her. Instead, she gave the land girl's meals, which consisted of cold fat bacon and beetroot, to her son to give to the land girl.

Poor food and unwelcoming billets were common. In July 1944 the *Sussex Express and County Herald* included a letter from an 'ex-land girl' in which she claimed that she had never received her full rations. Describing one billet, she wrote:

In the bedroom I occupied for nearly a year, all I had was one small drawer in which to keep my things, and the rest I kept in my case which I'd brought down from London with me...I don't think I ever got my full rations. I never saw a biscuit or syrup the whole time I was there, even though I had extra rations and points for threshing...I always got up to get my breakfast, and had my dinner to get ready as well...I think it is scandalous the way some of the landladies treat the girls. I, like many, came from London and had a very good home. I don't think my landlady wanted me in the first place. I preferred London and the 'blitz' to being put somewhere where I knew I was not wanted. (*Sussex Express* 28 July 1944)

The following week a landlady, describing herself as a 'soldier's wife' wrote a letter in defence of landladies generally, citing the difficulties of making rations stretch to meet the demands of 'the size of the average land girl's appetite'. Whatever the truth of this particular situation, it demonstrated clearly that there were instances where animosity was the order of the day.

Equally, however, many land girls remember farmers and farmers' wives who cooked well, were generous with rations and gave them hot drinks during cold weather, or hot water to make drinks. Some farmers also gave their land girls extra rations, such as watercress or eggs, either for themselves or to send home to families. Soldiers too, or searchlight operatives, often shared sandwiches and tea with land girls, and sometimes offered huge slabs of fruit cake, which were not available to most civilians during the war.

Caught Short

If facilities were basic in lodgings, they were non-existent in the fields, which could be embarrassing for shy women trying to find somewhere 'to go', particularly when men were working close by Some men were sensitive to women's needs but not always and land girls often had to hang on for as long as possible. Hazel King remembered:

> A lot of the trouble was when you wanted to spend a penny there were only the ditches. We used to manage because the men would go off but there was a time when, I think it was the Italians, they were there when we got there in the morning and they didn't go until late afternoon, and there was nowhere you could go. By the time they went home, you were nearly bursting. As they went off the field, there was a stampede to the ditches... .

The welfare officer arrived and on being told the problem came up with a solution – a type of portable loo; at least a shed with a toilet in it. However, Hazel and the other land girls were no better off because, 'the first morning it arrived and we went to see it, the Italians were in there cooking; they'd turned it into a kitchen'.

Often, when the call of nature hit, two land girls would go off together, so one could stand guard. Phyllis Cole, working as a thresher around Uckfield remembered, 'If we were in the fields, we'd be all right. One or two of you would hook up, and say "look there's a nice place behind that hedge" but if we wanted to go to the toilet, we would say to the farmer, "Can we use your toilet?" '

Some land girls, such as Blanche Lucas, recollect that going to the lavatory in the open air provided an opportunity for male workers to poke fun at them; something that they had to endure:

> There were one or two of them who were comedians. They used to say because we had nothing like toilets out there, we used to have to run away when we were working in the fields, hedging or ditching. This one farmer, he was a bit of a funny one. Two of us girls used to go off together and he used to shout after us, 'I know where you're going.' We all laughed really.

Isolated and Lonely

Although the public perception is that gaggles of land girls were employed on farms, the reality was frequently different. Many arrived on farms to find they were working on their own and were often billeted on their own. During her two years in the Land Army – she later left to join the ATS – Margaret Donaldson never worked with another land girl and was the only one in the village. Happily she got on well with the farmers that she worked for and formed a friendship with another land girl who was working, also on her own, in a nearby village. Helen Dawson worked on her own and there were many others in the same situation. Bernice Birch 'did feel isolated at times...towards the end of the war, it seemed so long [but] we did have contact with the organization. We had a meeting once a month.' Working on their own, land girls might have no one else to talk to for months, which was illustrated by an article sent to the *Land Girl* magazine in May 1940 by 'a Warwickshire Land Girl' and which described a trip she made to Birmingham, with other land girls, to be inspected by the Queen:

> I was picked up by car...and four of us went to Birmingham

he stained glass window in St Clements Church, Old Town Hastings was bombed during the
and the new one was dedicated to the war services. The model for the land girl (bottom left)
Betty Merrit, who served in the WLA from 1941–49, mainly as a tractor driver in East Sussex.

2a. Hazel King's (née Bannister) membership card for the WLA Club.

Women's Land Army Club

Membership Card

W.L.A. No. *116610*

Address *68 Military Rd*

Rye

Issued by Rye W.L.A. Club, Sussex

3a. Hazel's release certificate thanking her for her service to the WLA (1943–46).

WOMEN'S LAND ARMY (ENGLAND AND WALES).
RELEASE CERTIFICATE.

The Women's Land Army for England and Wales acknowledges with appreciation the services given by

Mrs. H.B.E. King.   W.L.A. 116610

who has been an enrolled member for the period from

10th May   19 43 to   11th December   19 46

and has this day been granted a willing release.

Date   11th December 1946.

COUNTY SECRETARY, WOMEN'S LAND ARMY.

4a. Cover of a Sussex WLA exhibition programme at the Corn Exchange, Brighton 1947.

W.L.A. EXHIBITION

CORN EXCHANGE
BRIGHTON
17th to 22nd FEBRUARY, 1947

Programme 1/-

Sussex Women's Land Army

EXHIBITION

CORN EXCHANGE

BRIGHTON

FEBRUARY 17th—22nd

1947

To be opened on Monday, February 17th at 3 p.m. by

HIS GRACE THE DUKE OF NORFOLK, K.G., P.C.

Agricultural Exhibits of W.L.A. Work
Arranged by the East Sussex W.A.E.C.

Ministry of Agriculture Exhibits

Trade Stalls   M.O.I. Films Daily 3 to 5 p.m.

W.L.A. Handicraft Display

Stalls - Fortune Teller - Sideshows - Teas - Music - Ices

Admission 1/- OPEN DAILY 2.30 to 8 p.m.

Children Half Price   W.L.A. in Uniform 6d.

The W.L.A. Entertains every Evening from 7 to 9 p.m.
in the Pavilion Theatre

Concerts - Plays - Brains Trust - Dance

For Further Information See Posters or Apply :

W.L.A. County Offices, 166 High St., Lewes and 31/32 West St., Horsham

---

Join the Women's Land Army and Help

E6766

Advert for the Sussex WLA exhibition in Brighton 1947, which included dancing, handicrafts and fortune telling.

THE WOMEN'S LAND ARMY BENEVOLENT FUND.

FUNDS RECEIVED BY MARCH 1st, 1947.

Raised by members and friends - - - over   £164,000
Grants by H.M. Treasury - - - - -   £160,000

The average number of grants made each month is 600.

LAND ARMY MEMBERS ARE HELPED WHEN NECESSARY IN THESE WAYS:—

Maintenance in sickness and when on compassionate leave.
Contribution towards maternity expenses.
Part payment of dental and optical bills.
Rehabilitation and training grants.
Free specialist's advice and assisted treatment for rheumatism.
Free independent legal advice in cases of accident.

THE FUND MAINTAINS:—

The Land Army Club where girls can stay in London.
Two Rest Break Houses by the sea.
35 beds at a country Convalescent Home.
A Homecraft Training Centre in Suffolk.

EX-MEMBERS OF THE LAND ARMY may also apply to the Fund for help in time of special hardship.

Applications should be sent through the Land Army office of the county in which the member or ex-member works or lives.

5a. Flyer for the WLA Benevolent Fund, which was set up in 1942 to assist land girls suffering financial hardship. The British government did not give land girls the same post-war support as women in other services, notably Civil Defence and the ATS. Following an outcry, the government gave £150,000 to the Fund.

7a. WLA badge with its wheatsheaf motif.

8a. The same motif is repeated on the banner of the *Land Army News*.

LAND ARMY NEWS

| Vol. I. | MARCH 1948 | No. 10. |

EDITORIAL NOTES

AT this season of the year work on the land begins to increase and as they get that springtime feeling, some members of the Land Army begin to wish they knew a bit more about what lies behind their work. Most of us realise that there is a very good reason for doing even the dullest job and if we knew that reason much of the backache and heartache would be removed.

For those with high educational qualifications the way is comparatively simple through a university or college degree or diploma course. For the rest, who have no desire to fly so high but would still like to improve their knowledge of farming, there are two ways open. Each year the Ministry of Agriculture allots to the Land Army a certain number of training vacancies under the Vocational Training Scheme. These vacancies are available for members with a minimum of two years' satisfactory service who wish to make a career in agriculture or horticulture and who are capable of assimilating the theoretical and laboratory instruction given at the training centres. Students take a written examination at the end of the course and a certificate is awarded to successful candidates. Several hundreds of Land Army Members have passed through these

SUCCESS STORIES

We report the following:—

Hants. E. K. Field, 56350, is still wearing gum boots issued in November, 1941. They have been in frequent use all the time.

Norfolk. 22 Land girls lifted 87 tons of carrots in 6½ days. The farmer was so pleased with their work that he has asked for their services from April onwards.

Warwickshire. Twenty girls from Wolverton Court Hostel working at Thelsford, completed the potato picking so quickly and successfully that their employer arranged for them all to go to the Shakespeare Memorial Theatre, in Stratford-on-Avon, to see a performance of "The New Moon."

W. Suffolk. Ten Land girls and six men threshed, carted and stacked 103 sacks of yeoman wheat in 6½ hours. The most remarkable fact about this achievement was that seven out of the ten Land girls were new recruits.

N. Wales. E. Jones, 103855 who has hitherto been known to us as a good all-round worker with a special emphasis on calf rearing has started a spare time poultry enterprise on her own. Out of 100 cockerels she bought in October, 98 are still alive and her 100 day old pullets, also bought in October are due to lay any day. She is adding to her stock by 100 per cent. in the spring.

HAVE A GO

At 3.30 p.m. the great day began for the girls of the W.L.A. Hostel Pollington, the show for which they had waited for weeks was just about to start. There was an audience of about 300 friends to "Have a Go" with Wilfred Pickles, and did they have a go?

For about an hour and a half before the recording began the girls were entertained by celebrities whom Wilfred brought with him

We had a great surprise when the "Big White Chief" as Wilfred called our Warden, walked on to the stage. Wilfred wished her the best of luck as she will be leaving shortly to get married. She caused great merriment by saying her favourite drink is champagne and her greatest ambition to have two boys and a girl. Miss Kenden answered questions on gardening, her favourite hobby, collected her money and made way for the next contestant amid loud cheers, from her (good) girls.

Margaret McNicholas, who hails from Rotherham, followed; she caused great joviality all through her turn. She has a very deep voice and the audience was much amused when she said her favourite nick-name is "Porky" because she is on the plump side. She answered questions on personalities and received 38s. 6d. from "the man with the money."

Then came Flossie White in full uniform, complete with hat. Flossie told Wilfred she would rather have been a boy than a girl so that she could indulge in her favourite hobbies which are cobbling and carpentry. She answered questions on Land Army songs and we all joined in and "Give her the money Barney" was there again.

May Green was last on the programme, everybody laughed when they heard she would like to be "Eve in the garden of Eden" and like other volunteers, she won her money.

The show ended with Wilfred Pickles shouting "Cheerio everybody" and the strains of the signature tune ringing out once again. "Have a Go" will live long in the memories of those at Pollington Hostel.

PASTURES NEW

Berkshire. Girl required to take complete charge of kitchen garden to be run as market

WLA armband and badge. A half diamond denoted six months' service.

. The red and green colours are reversed in this version of the WLA armband.

11a. WLA doll made by Mrs M. Culling of Kennington on display at the Brenzett Aeronautical Museum, a former WLA hostel.

12a–13a. WLA Christmas card.

Be gentle when you touch bread,
Let it not lie uncared for, unwanted,
Too often bread is taken for granted.
There is such beauty in bread,
Beauty of sun and soil,
Beauty of patient toil,
Wind and rain have caressed it,
Christ often blessed it.
Be gentle when you touch bread.

To Hazel, wishing you a very happy Christmas From Margery.

14a. Wooden ashtray made by German POWs at Robertsbridge and owned by former land girl Blanche Lucas.

Part of the WLA display at Brenzett, a former WLA hostel, now part of Brenzett Aeronautical Museum, Romney Marsh, Kent.

16a. This display of farming implements at Brenzett Aeronautical Museum includes a milk churn which land girls were expected to move around when full of milk. Former land girl Beryl Peacha describes having to tip milk churns slightly to one side then edge them along because they were heavy to carry.

together. How we talked! I had not seen anyone else in the Land Army for months, and it was great to talk over all our experiences...

Isolated land girls were not only lonely but also had to struggle with unfamiliar tasks, hard backbreaking work, or make mistakes, without support or encouragement from others going through the same initiation. In June 1940 five land girls, who were working on a farm in West Riding and sharing a cottage, wrote to the *Land Girl* magazine describing their lives. They had no doubt about the benefits of working with others: 'Life together, when there are five, is great fun. Such accidents as falling in the midden in the snow, falling off our tricycles, or breakdowns of the vans, are of little importance when we can laugh over them together...'

Not for the Land Army are the community existence, the parades, the marchings-past, the smart drill, the eyes-right, the salutes-or very seldom. For the most part its members work isolated and in a mouse-like obscurity. Their very uniform seems to suggest a bashful camouflage of green-and-fawn to be lost against the grass or the stubble...instead of her silks and georgettes she wears wool and corduroy and clumping boots; her working-hours seem never definitely to end...she lives among strangers, and the jolly atmosphere of homely love or outside fun is replaced often by loneliness and boredom...

(Vita Sackville-West, *The Women's Land Army*)

The *Land Girl*

Lady Gertrude Denman and other WLA organizers were only too aware of the problems of isolation, which is why the *Land Girl* magazine was started. Its aims were to provide a link between isolated workers, to encourage *esprit de corps* and to provide news of other land girls and the organization.

The *Land Girl* was published once a month from April 1940. Its editor was Mrs Margaret Pyke, a remarkable woman who, like Lady Denman, was closely associated with the family planning movement and was one of the founder members of what was later known as the Family Planning Association. The Margaret

Pyke Centre in London is named after her.

Every month the *Land Girl* was packed with news, letters and articles from land girls. Margaret Pyke wrote the editorial which usually focused on a relevant topic and land girls and lumber jills were invited to send in contributions by the 27th of each month at the latest, in order to meet printing deadlines. The magazine included photographs, knitting patterns, recipes, humorous pieces, short stories and competitions, one of which encouraged land girls to submit essays on 'Wartime Adaptability'. A section entitled 'News from the Counties' kept 'people who are tucked away on isolated farms in touch with all the Land Army doings' and included news from every county from weddings through to talks, rallies, parties, concerts, and Land Army success stories. 'News from the Counties' was obviously widely read although one poignant comment from East Suffolk land girls in August 1940 stated that, 'We read with envy of all the meetings and rallies held in other counties, but here volunteers are so scattered that it has not been practical to emulate them...'

Lady Denman contributed the occasional piece, as did the Minister of Agriculture, Robert Hudson, and trade union representatives. The Queen too, as WLA patron, sent a regular Christmas message and, as war progressed, farmers sent in commendations. The magazine was very popular. It cost 3d and eventually reached a circulation of some 21,000. It ended in March 1947 and was replaced by a free broadsheet, *Land Army News*, which continued until 1950.

Welfare and Community Activities

Land Army representatives, or reps as they were known, were responsible for checking on the wellbeing of land girls in their area, making regular visits to ensure that billets, work and living conditions were suitable, investigating any complaints and arranging transfers if conditions on a farm or in billets were unsuitable. They also had the unenviable or exasperating task of sorting out disagreements between farmers and land girls or with landladies, who sometimes found land girls difficult to deal with. The reps were also supposed to provide their local charges with advice and information about joining public libraries, meetings of the Women's Institute, and how to get involved with organizations such as the Young Women's Christian Association, and the local vicar and so on. Volunteers were assured that they would not just be put on a farm and then be forgotten by the County headquarters.

According to the *Land Army Manual*, the local rep would 'try to make her [volunteer] as happy as possible in her new surroundings...will explain...the amenities of the village or country town...the postal facilities, local or county libraries...the nearest doctor, chemists, shops...'

At their best, WLA reps worked hard to help their charges to settle and even invited them to their homes; they were, of course, from a very different class, which could be a source of amusement as Peggy Pearce describes:

> When we were in Englefield Green we had a Lady something who came to see us. She rode a bicycle and she always had a long black skirt. She'd come to see 'her gels'. She was very nice, lived in a beautiful house and she had us there to have a bath. She'd say, 'How are my gels?' and then 'I wonder what the time is' and she'd pick her skirt up and her watch was in her pocket in her pants. Oh, she was so funny.

Class differences could cause tensions and not all WLA reps were sympathetic to their young charges, something that Vita Sackville-West, herself a WLA rep in Kent, touched on in her book *The Women's Land Army*. She devoted quite a large section to the rep's work, describing it as 'not always enviable' and one requiring 'considerable tact and sympathy'. She appears to have tried to be even-handed but nevertheless stated that land girls could be 'unbearably tiresome' and at times 'downright ill-behaved', which was, no doubt, true at times, and at the same time recognized that reps came from the more privileged classes and that 'some divergence...must inevitably arise between the staid squirearchy of middle-age and gay wild youth out for all the fun it can get'. This last comment, however, suggests that her sympathies may have tended towards women of her own class.

Land girls were encouraged to use local libraries and attend any classes or lectures that the county representative might organize. Rallies were sometimes organized to which all WLA girls within easy distance would be invited. According to the *Manual*, 'food is sometimes provided and a good time had by all'. However the *Manual* went on to say, 'It must not be thought that the Land Girl is constantly going about on trips but it does make for *esprit de corps*...it does give a girl a feeling of being a member of an important army...'

A land girl was advised that 'she can do much to make her own life happy if she tries to make others happy too...' As well as getting involved with village life, land girls were also urged to do voluntary work such as lending a hand with the local Air Raid Precaution (ARP) and fire watch. A surprising number did involve themselves in other activities but, given the long hours and gruelling workload, the advice was not always practical even if well meant.

Living in Hostels

The contrast between women who lived and worked on their own, and those who lived in hostels, was striking. Stella Hope, for instance, remembered vividly how difficult it was for her on her own and how much her life changed when she was finally placed in a WLA hostel. The WLA recognized that billets and lodgings were often not ideal and decided that hostels would be a good way of overcoming loneliness and improving their living conditions. The WLA commandeered a wide range of dwellings from country houses through to stables and converted them into living accommodation for land girls. They also built hostels, including the one in Brenzett, Kent, which has been restored by Ray Brignall, and is the only surviving WLA hostel in the southeast. It housed 48 land girls, who slept in small dormitory like units, 4 bunk beds to a unit. Each land girl had her own wardrobe and a set of drawers for clothes. The hostel contained a laundry room, bathroom, sick room and communal sitting room, with a piano. Permanent staff cooked, cleaned and maintained the hostel, which was run by a matron. By 1944, there were nearly 700 Land Army hostels in existence, providing living accommodation for about 22,000 land girls. Rules were strict and land girls had to be indoors by 10 p.m.

One land girl who had lived in Gloucester and was sent to a WLA hostel in Kent, remembered that:

> We had great fun, we had two pianos in the hostel and Matron used to sit down and she used to play hymns and some classical stuff and one girl in there, Vera Rose, she could play anything. We used to like to dance and that, and so to get rid of Matron, somebody had a bright idea. They went to the phone box at the top of the land and phoned her and she [Matron] went to the office to answer the phone and, of course, the other girls were on the piano…we used to have fun, great fun…

Another woman who loved hostel life was June Ivy Merritt. She joined the Land Army in 1947, worked in a gang and was sent to a hostel in Edenbridge:

> I adored it. I'd got people to talk to [and] no Mum. I was doing all sorts of farm work, working in a gang organized by the War Ag. We used to do anything. Being the youngest one and not knowing anything about the work, they dropped me off at this farm and left me. I went and knocked on the farmhouse door and this woman said: 'Oh, do come in', she said, 'We've been expecting you, we're just going on holiday and you're taking over.' She said, 'You have been to agricultural college, haven't you?' and I said, 'No, I only joined this week.'

Sheelah Cruttenden's children believe that a land girl's experience depended on where they were sent. Their mother lived in a hostel: 'It depended where you were stationed. Mum knew someone who was on her own for the whole war, and it was a completely different experience for her so I think she was lucky that she was with all these others; that was probably what made it.' Their mother was sent to a hostel in Warwickshire, and wrote:

The second hostel I lived in was the rather magnificent Dumbleton Hall in the village of Dumbleton, Worcestershire. Apparently the Nazi Ambassador Baron von Ribbentrop had visited the Hall before the war and gave such a good impression of it to his leader that Hitler made plans to use it for his personal home in the event of a successful invasion. Lord and Lady Monsell owned the Hall...the WLA used most of the ground floor and some of the rooms at the top of the house...At Dumbleton all the girls were field workers. They were organized into gangs and sent out to farms that had requested labour. Gangs were transported to work in a WAEC (Worcestershire Agricultural Executive Committee) truck. Work involved mainly threshing in the winter months and also included hoeing, singling, picking up, pulling sugar beet, picking out wild oats, harvesting and sorting potatoes.

After paying for my lodgings I was left with about 11s 7d, out of which came money for essential items such as washing powder, soap, towels, shampoo and stamps. My sister and I remember taking washing home for our Mum to do at weekends which was then sent back to us through the post! The girls were provided with a decent breakfast, fried bread and baked beans was a particularly well-remembered meal. Cereal and porridge were also available in the hostels breakfast room. A hot dinner was provided at the end of the day: however the girls provided their own sandwiches to eat in the fields. The girls were given a pot of jam each month. At the cry of 'Jam's out', a stampede ensued with the girls desperate to avoid being left with the less tasty varieties! That was the first time that I remember eating a 'Weetabix', which I took to work dry with jam spread on it. For drinks the gangs were given a screw of tea and sugar and were provided with hot water by the farmer.

Work finished by five o'clock although in certain cases overtime was available – gladly taken on in the freshness of the morning but viewed with less relish by the end of the day. The hostel had a ten o'clock curfew. Up until then the girls were able to please themselves after work.

Hostel life did not suit everyone nor was it necessarily available to all. In October 1942, the *Land Girl* published an article entitled 'Hostels or Billets' in which it argued that both types of living accommodation had advantages:

> ...hostels offer greater opportunities for community life and amusement, billets give greater peace and quiet, freedom from regulations and a much better opportunity for those who live in them to become part of the neighbouring community.

Whether those who were living in isolated lodgings would have agreed is debatable.

Hostels provided companionship and many women made close friendships that lasted well beyond the war. According to Audrey Blythe:

> It was a great life, it was one of the best things I've ever done. You made the best friends you'll ever have. You don't make friends like that now. If one girl had a date, the others would mill around, one would perm her hair. You'd share, that's the way it was and if you misbehaved, you'd get chucked in a bath of cold water. We had plenty of energy as I remember. We used to finish work, jump on a bike and cycle to Sandwich to have a swim.

Land girls living and working on their own often envied the camaraderie enjoyed by those in hostels or working in gangs, but some managed to strike up acquaintances with other land girls, or form friendships in the villages or with the farming community.

Working with the Enemy

The British Government put prisoners of war (POWs) to work on the land, where they provided a valuable work force. They were sometimes treated better than the land girls themselves. Most land girls worked alongside German or Italian prisoners of war, which was initially a strange experience, as Sheelah Cruttenden described:

I remember the Italians were particularly fond of scented soap, a commodity they asked for in place of money for the wooden toys and string slippers that they made. I also remember working with German POWs. An awkward situation overcome only after the initial shock of 'working with the enemy' had worn off.

Based in Kent, Eileen Hodd worked with POWs and found them very friendly:

I worked with three German POWs. They were extremely nice, very polite, one always called me 'Miss Eileen'; he almost clicked his heels together when we spoke. One was an older man, Hermann, he didn't have any family, just his wife and when he talked about her, he would almost cry, he would go away from you and kneel down and pray, and then there was Otto. I suppose he was about my age, a little bit of flirting I suppose but they were extremely pleasant. When you work with people, they really didn't seem any different from anybody else; you couldn't really be prejudiced against them because they were always very, very pleasant and very polite. One had two sons; he showed me photographs and there used to be a gang of German prisoners that used to work in the woods cutting pit props. They used to make toys out of wood. It was a straight piece of wood, a little man carved and a piece of string and when you squeezed the bottom of the wood, the little man would jump over, and also another square with a handle and a little chicken carved on the top with a piece of string tied through holes with a weight on the bottom and when you swung the weight, the little chicken used to peck. Fascinating they were.

After the war, Eileen married a soldier who had been billeted in her village but he died tragically in a farm accident soon afterwards. One of the prisoners of war whom she had met during the war sent her a 'very lovely condolence card because they heard what had happened'.

Tractor-driver Hazel King also worked with prisoners of war:

At one time we had these young Germans, they were a bit different and we were a bit uppity, we didn't want to work with them and they were quite nice to us apart from the fact that they would catch mice and put them in your pocket; they were young like us. The Italians and Russians were older than us and they were all right – we couldn't understand what they said but we could make each other understand and they came and picked up potatoes.

Stella Hope

Memories of the Land Army

Within a couple of weeks, I received my uniform and was asked to go for an interview at a farm in Hartley near to Cranbrook. Nobody I saw gave me any information as to what I would be doing or the hours I would be working, but I was told to report on the Monday morning at 7 a.m. I was then told to go and find an address, which would be my billet. This was a two up and two down cottage. I was shown a bedroom with a single bed and a dressing table of four drawers and a small standing mirror. Next to this was a washstand, on which were a bowl, jug and a bucket underneath. That was all the furniture within this room. Clothes that needed to be hung up were just put on a hook on the door.

I was supposed to catch the 8 p.m. bus from Maidstone on the Sunday evening to get to the billet by about 9 p.m., then things started to go wrong. The bus timetable had been changed and the only bus going that evening was at 10 p.m. - I arrived late. I was tired and hungry by the time I arrived, and of course, was dying to go to the 'loo'. I asked where it was; 'Outside in the yard', I was told. Off I went, happy to be able to relieve myself - I had never before seen a chemical closet, and was looking around for the chain to flush said toilet. That brought on a snigger, I can tell you. After which we all went to bed, that is the two occupants of the cottage and myself went to bed, no supper - these people were in the habit of going to bed at 9 p.m. at the latest. I had no idea where to wash, but I soon found out in the morning, I had a jug of water, and that was it!

Next morning I was woken up at 6 a.m., ugh - I washed to the best of my ability, and was given a slice of toast [and] a packet, for my lunch, which contained a chunk of bread and a lump of cheese. Also a bottle of cold tea. I very shortly began to enjoy these things, but not at first. I was directed to a bicycle, very old and very dirty, but nevertheless workable. I followed the man of the house down a county lane, very rickety and very stony. Waiting at the farm was the Manager and two other men. Everybody reported to him at 7 a.m. to be given their jobs for the day.

I was taken for what felt like a very long hike to a hop field, and instructed to tie hop strings into bunches of four. Simple enough, but in the other part of the field the other men were working, stringing up to the hop wires. On the other side of the field there were the enemy (or so I thought), they were twenty or so German prisoners of war, doing a job called twiddling. This meant they had to twist the hop bines up on the hop strings. This was my first introduction, but the worst thing was, how was I going to 'wee'? I hadn't any idea. I suffered until lunchtime and made a bolt for the chem toilet, bliss.

Gradually I was introduced to quite a few other jobs, but generally I found that if there was a particularly nasty job, then the expression was 'give it to the girl'. One of the worst jobs was cleaning out the chicken pens; I never ever saw a man do this job.

Some of the hardest jobs were the loneliest. I had to dig out a load of dung from a cattle pen, miles from anywhere; this was where cattle were kept during the winter. When the cattle were in I had to walk down and get water out of the river to fill their water tank. That was fine but when the river was frozen over and the ice had to be broken, that hurt; the water was very cold and so were my hands, but it had to be done, no point in crying.

On one particular morning, I was doing one of my regular jobs, walking for miles or so it seemed, counting the cattle, and making sure the fences were all in good order. I discovered that one of the cows had slipped a calf, the poor little thing didn't look at all well to my mind; remember now that I was a novice. So what did I do? I picked up the calf and started to walk back to the farm, which was a good mile away. All of a sudden I heard a thundering of hooves, and there was right at my shoulder was the Mum cow. Whoops.

I carried on, with this cow, literally breathing over my shoulder, watching every move I made. It wasn't till I got to the farm that I was told I could have been killed, apparently cows charge with their eyes open, unlike bulls that charge with their eyes shut. But I got away with it. Mum must have thought her calf was in no danger.

I learned the hard way, there are no regular hours in farming, the double summer time was in and if there was a job to be done, then it was done, whatever the time.

One incident that I constantly think of in regard to this farm, which was, of course, the first that I worked on - people are not as nice as they appear. There was one (for want of a better word) gentleman, who was cruel to animals; I think he was scared of them. He and I had to take out the horse and cart, to get a load of hay. I was told by him to cut the hay. OK. - he wasn't going to do the job - the cutter is a huge curved blade, which had to slice through the hay in the stack. What wouldn't I have given for Health and Safety. Whilst I was doing this, the man kept striking the horse and, of course, eventually the horse got fed up - and bolted. He went through three gates, breaking them into bits, and through fields. I was left to try to catch the poor beast.

On my 21st birthday, the rain was coming down in torrents, but bless me, the farmer wanted some potatoes dug. I was out in the field, doing this filthy job, and it was filthy, because of the rain, and it was my birthday, and nobody remembered me. Oh misery me.

It comes back to me that I had no place to do any laundry, but I remember that I always took everything home with me to wash. I was much too shy to ask for anything, so perhaps it was my fault, but with hindsight, I would have thought that somebody would have told me where to do these chores.

After about 18 months of general farming, I went to the Hostel at Lake House, Staplehurst, which was a very nice Tudor type house, in quiet grounds. There were only about 16 girls there. For a few weeks I worked alongside 'the gang' - girls who used to go out together, driven by truck to different farms to do all kinds of jobs. One of these was tree felling, heavy work, but we were assisted, once again by German prisoners of war.

I then went on to bailing hay and straw, once again this was a very dirty job but could be lots of fun, working with other girls. Although we were expected to stack the bales of straw or hay in the barns, not an easy task, I can assure you.

When you are working as what was known as private, it was exceptionally lonely, whereas most of the girls in the Hostel went out in groups, to the pictures or skating, I didn't get much of a chance, unless we were 'rained off'. You can imagine that we got excited if it did rain, and no other jobs could be found.

For a change, two of us went to Cumberland, at Gosforth. Now this was a different type of farming. Up hill and down dale. But quite pleasant, once your legs got used to the different types of territory.

One of the nicest meals I had was on one of the farms up there. The farmer asked us (there were three of us) what had we got in our food tins. We showed him and he was disgusted; it was sliced bread and whatever we had put on it, paste or jam. He told us not to eat 'that muck'. About ten minutes later he came out of the farmhouse with some newly baked bread, fresh butter and blackcurrant jam. AND a jug of hot tea. One other farmer, up there, in Cumberland always made sure we had a large glass of milk. But this was a rarity.

After three months I went back to Staplehurst and worked on the threshers and bailers. This, once again, was heavy work and, of course, in the long summer days, the hours were long. The first time I got on top of one of these monsters, I was very afraid but then one doesn't get scared, not if you want to keep face. But very shortly I became quite used to it. I could tell by the tone of the drum whether or not things were going on OK. I found that the worse things to thresh were flax, or barley with lots of thistles in.

Some of the farmers were quite nice but there was those who were, to say the least, absolute pigs. They treated you as second-class citizens... I remember once pulling in a farm with the bailer and the men brought in the thresher at about 4.30 p.m. We set up the machinery ready for an early start in the morning, but that wasn't good enough for this particular farmer; he wanted us to start up straight away irrespective of the fact that we had finished on one farm and brought the machinery to his place.

In the mornings we had an earlier start than most; the machinery had to be greased and got ready for work. The box in which the feeder stood was made up of straw bundles and made comfortable as could be because you would be standing there all day apart from meal breaks.

One of the dirtiest tricks played on me when I first worked on the threshers was when I finished up in the evening and went to put my coat on. I put my hand in my pocket and, lo and behold, it was full of mice; the men had collected them up and put them in. They thought they would upset me; they did, but I wouldn't let them see it.

A very scary time I had when I was taking a bailer up Hunton Hill, there were a lot of children chasing behind the bailer and I was worried about changing gear in case the bailer rolled back - very frightening.

I finished up at Sissinghurst, where I worked on a combine harvester. Another filthy job. I was [also] sent out with a tractor, which must have come out of the Ark. It was so old and not very well maintained. I worked with this thing nearly all day long, harrowing the ground but then it failed. I couldn't get the thing started again. I swung the handle for what seemed forever, until my tummy ached with the pain of it. I had to walk back to the home farm and tell them what happened, that the tractor was in the field. I went by that farm about two years later and it was still there. Whoops.

Some farmers could be quite insulting and others treated you with a kind of respect, but most of the time you were just there. The jobs had to be done and you had volunteered so - get on with it. The money was very poor. In the hostels, laundry had to be paid for and there were no concessions with regard to fares on buses or trains, although you were allowed four travel warrants a year. The advantage of living in the hostels [was] not only for the company, but there were BATHS, wowee.

* * *

Chapter 8

Acceptance and Prejudice

*T*he men with whom I worked on this farm had taken a bet that I
wouldn't last three months especially as I was used to working in
London as a very junior secretary.

(Stella Hope)

MANY land girls play down the amount of prejudice
they encountered during the war but it certainly
existed – and there are stories to prove it. Farmers
often resented the fact that land girls were foisted onto them,
some of their wives viewed land girls with suspicion or even
jealousy, and villagers and country people were often not very
welcoming to inexperienced young women, who arrived from
towns and cities, ignorant of country ways in general, and
farming in particular.

Offering Advice

Both the *Land Girl* magazine and *Land Army Manual* offered
advice about how best to fit into the country, even though it frequently exposed a somewhat stereotypical view of the lives of
town and city young women. The *Manual* devoted an entire
chapter to 'Making the most of the country' and aimed it in particular at 'the town girl [who] does not often find it easy to live
in the country'. The chapter assumed that the 'town girl':

> …misses the amenities…cannot pop into the local cinema,
> cannot even go round the local fish-and-chip shop…[is] not
> able to stroll down the High Street and have a look at the

shops and there are not, of course, the number of men about to go to dances with at the local Palais de Dance...

This last was not always quite true, given the number of soldiers who were often stationed in the countryside.

In particular the *Manual* warned city-born women against labelling country folk as 'country bumpkins' or 'old fashioned' and, taking a rather defensive tack, told the new recruits in no uncertain terms that country folk '...usually know far more than those who are bred and born in cities and towns...[they]...may not know the names of the film stars...but they do know the names of the birds...can tell the weather...they have a different kind of knowledge...'

The *Manual* went on to urge land girls to see the 'other fellow's point of view', remarking that 'she will only be stared at if she wears her latest Bond Street creation at the local hop...or is constantly boasting of her doings in town...' and strongly advised them to show consideration for the farmer's land and family, to always be willing to give a helping hand, to be punctual, not to smoke around the place, to shut gates behind them, and to put tools away properly. In essence, the *Manual* said loud and clear that 'Farmers have no time to bother with fussy volunteers'. Instead they expected 'girls who have offered to do the work to carry it out without complaint...'

The *Land Girl* magazine reiterated the advice. In July 1940, under the heading 'Helping the Farmer', Land Army workers were told to effectively keep their mouths shut, and watch carefully what was going on around them. In particular, women were told to: '...trim those long nails down a bit – and whilst you are at it, I should leave the nail polish off for a day or two...it does look a bit more workmanlike to turn out all natural for once...' In addition, they were advised that 'the farmer really has not got time to listen to your experiences on the pier at Brighton last year...'

The issue of whether land girls should use cosmetics while working on the farm came up more than once. Not only the *Manual* but also the *Land Girl* and Vita Sackville-West raised the issue. In October 1940, the *Land Girl* ran a piece asking the burning question: 'Should Land Girls use make-up?' and answered it, not surprisingly, as follows:

> This can only be a matter for personal decision, but perhaps it is worth remembering that (a) make-up on the farm is much more conspicuous than in a town; and (b) country people are much less used to make-up than town folk…

Cosmetics and farms obviously were not seen as compatible, and for those who might have been reluctant to appear in the morning with a face free of make-up, the *Manual* offered the reassuring information that within a very short space of time, outdoor working would give the women such glowing complexions that they would not need to use rouge anyway.

Prejudice and Resentment

In some ways, the instructions, although meant to be helpful, were harsh and they reveal a somewhat patronizing attitude towards what were seen as frivolous town-bred young women. This perhaps reflects the background and class of the WLA officials and organizers, who were in the main county women from the privileged land-owning classes. Vita Sackville-West's comments about troublesome and difficult land girls fall into that category, and there were tensions between working-class land girls and their more privileged representatives. There could also be tensions between land girls from different social backgrounds as Blanche Lucas remembered:

> We did have a local organizer who came occasionally, or there was a place we could go, her house in the area. One was Miss Debenham and she was Debenham and Freebody, they were in the county town and they had these representatives around but they were all in the big houses. I didn't meet any upper-class girls; there were a couple of them, a bit snooty. They tried to be superior but it didn't go down very well, we didn't take any notice.

Given the patronizing attitudes, it is extraordinary the extent to which most land girls, particularly those from towns and cities, took on their unfamiliar tasks without complaint and worked as hard as humanly possible to bring in harvests, plough up land, care for animals and ensure the nation's food and timber supplies, often in appalling conditions.

> We had one farmer, his name was de Gros, and he was a marvellous boss. If we worked overtime, he'd pay us in our hand. He had to feed us and bring us back home. We had a whale of a time with him.
>
> (Audrey Blythe)

The way farmers behaved towards the land girls varied enormously. Some were good employers; they showed land girls what to do, were sympathetic or amused when mistakes occurred, made land girls feel welcome and appreciated their efforts. But this was not always the case. Land girls who were employed in their own locality, often by farmers they already knew, had few problems but there were others who had very bad experiences. Phyllis Cole, who worked as a thresher with other land girls, moving from farm to farm, found that most of the farmers she worked for were good employers and appreciative of their work. She vividly remembered one farmer who provided them with a shed, a bavin (bunch of kindling twigs) to make a fire to boil water for tea, and even showed them his prizes for beef cattle. But on another occasion, she worked for a farmer who was far less caring:

> We went to another farm and it was snowing and after a while, when it gets too wet, the belt starts slipping and you have to pack it in. Well, it started to snow, I was up on the top cutting and I thought to myself, 'Cor, we're not going to be up here much longer'. Anyway, he wasn't a very nice farmer. At lunchtime he brought a cup of hot tea out for his men, but he ignored us. I said 'Don't we get a cup then?' He said, 'You don't work for me, you're just girls.' He hadn't got a very high opinion of women. Now in the finish, it got so cold there and of course we hadn't had any hot tea and I was on the top, I passed out. Well he got the wind up then, he got his son to take me home in the car, which he had to...

For Phyllis this was a one-off occurrence, but instances like this were repeated up and down the country and there were many land girls who were neglected, bullied or even sexually harassed by farmers or male agricultural workers. Many women felt that as land girls they were given the worst jobs and that their harsh treatment was gender-biased; male workers would not, in their view, have been treated in the same way.

Pamela McDowell, 88, was a land girl in Kent during 1944-45. Like others she had both good and bad experiences. Most of the men she encountered on farms were helpful but not all of them. She believed that some male workers just resented working with women and, as a result, she, like many of the other land girls, worked twice as hard to prove herself:

> We were all equal. We had to do exactly the same, we couldn't expect them [men] to come and say, 'Oh, I'll help you little woman', we were one of the workers. I did everything they did. I worked alongside the men. You were very adaptable, you just fall in with whatever's going on.
>
> (Margaret Donaldson)

I think that on the whole the War Ag officers respected us and were reasonably satisfied with the standard of our work. But not all the male farm labourers would have agreed. Many of them resented us and lost no opportunity to tell us how useless we were and that we were only fit to do the most routine and boring jobs. I used to argue, unrealistically, that there were very few jobs that we couldn't manage but it always came down to the matter of strength – lifting tractor tow bars or cranking the old Fordson tractors…

I can remember some really unpleasant farm workers who made the job pretty difficult for us, but there were many more who were helpful and encouraging. Of course many of the younger farm hands had gone into the Forces and I don't think that many farmers would have employed land girls if the men had been available, but they were on the whole appreciative of our efforts, though few would have made any concessions to make the job easier for us – we had taken the place of the men and were expected to do the jobs as they would have done them…

…I had frequent arguments with some of the more macho

types, who liked to put the girls down... There was one occasion when I was challenged to carry a hundredweight sack of corn across the barn. It was a wet day and we were all inside mending sacks or some such wet weather task...I was determined to show that I could do it, so they hoisted the sack onto my shoulders and I started to walk across the floor. My knees began to buckle but I was not going to give in and somehow I managed to get to the other side... (Pamela McDowell's private papers, 'Memories of the Women's Land Army in Kent 1944-45', with permission)

> Some farmers were bad. Some treated you as if you were something on their shoe and you were just something there to do the slavery. They wouldn't treat the men like that.
>
> (Stella Hope)

For some land girls, prejudice or sexism from farmers was not a problem. Blanche Lucas, for instance, never experienced sexism. She knew that some farmers 'could be nasty' but she was lucky in that she was accepted. She had been born and brought up on a farm and was used to the farm life so 'it was no hardship to me'. The men she worked with 'wouldn't treat a lady badly' and she got on well with them, but she knew it was different for others:

...Some girls came from the north and London and never having had any experience of the hard work...this is why the farmers said at the outbreak of the war 'They'll never manage it, they'll never do a man's job'. I think towards the end they changed their mind, but there were still a few farmers who resented ladies, I think they resented it...

When Beryl Peacham joined the Land Army she continued to work with her mother on the farm, Grandturzel, where they lived. Together they did all the work on the farm, from milking, cleaning out the cowsheds, thistle cutting, ploughing and even lifting heavy 2¼ cwt sacks of wheat up from the ground and onto a trailer. Farmers living close by were helpful and released some of their male workers to help during particularly busy times; they also had help from Canadian soldiers who were billeted near Burwash. Being a member of the farming community, she personally did not experience sexism or prejudice from male workers, but she remembered that, '…when land girls first went to the farms, a lot of the farm workers said: 'Urgh, they won't last, too thin and no muscles' and all that sort of thing. Some farmers thought the girls wouldn't be able to do the work when the Land Army first started.'

Cruelty and Sexual Harassment

Land girls experienced sexual harassment and also saw instances of cruelty that were hard to deal with. Interestingly, some land girls were more concerned about the way animals were treated than themselves. Peggy Pearce was sent to one farm in Shamley Green in Surrey where she encountered difficulties with the farm manager:

> The farm people were all right but I didn't like the farm manager; he was ginger haired and wanted to put his arm around you, I didn't like him one little bit and he was a cruel man. I went absolutely mental. The cows kept on getting out into the next farm where the cabbages were, so you can imagine how popular that was; they ate all the cabbages and he whacked them with sticks to get them in and it really made me see red. Absolutely furious I was and I said 'If you looked after your hedges properly that wouldn't happen' and he was still whacking them. We got into the cowshed [and] on the wall was a big strap. I got hold of this strap and I absolutely whacked him with it, and I said, 'That's it'. He thought he was going to carry on with me but I had great objections to him. I wasn't very happy and I was in rotten digs. He didn't get anywhere with me, he was very disappointed and then, whatever I did, he thought was wrong. I used to cut across the fields to go to my digs and on the way I'd pick mushrooms. He told me off saying, 'You should take these to the farmhouse; they're not yours.' Whatever he could find wrong, he did, so I wasn't happy there.

Apparently a land girl who had previously worked on the same farm had left because of the farm manager, and so too did

126

Peggy. She did not make a formal complaint, although she knew this was possible, but telephoned the county organizers. A rep came out to see her and she was transferred to another farm.

Sexist attitudes were widespread in the farming community, which was hardly surprising in such a male-dominated environment and macho culture. Very few land girls describe themselves as feminists – which would have been surprising anyway in the 1940s – but, nevertheless, few had any doubts that male farm workers had little respect for the land girls because they were women.

> I think some of the women resented the fact that we could do a man's job but it wasn't that we were doing a man's job, we were taking the place of a man who was fighting.
>
> (Phyllis Cole)

Land girls were also attacked and there were instances of rape or attempted rape. On 29 May 1942, the *Sussex Express and County Herald* reported an assault on a land girl by a soldier. The land girl, who left the pub with her attacker, was thrown to the ground, hit in the face, and the soldier pulled a knife on her. Passers by came to her rescue. The case came to court where evidence was presented as to the soldier's previous good record and, perhaps not surprisingly, the soldier was let off with only a fine.

Changing Attitudes

As war progressed, land girls themselves seem to have had some effect, for the better, on the sexism within farming, even though it would not have been expressed that way at the time. Whether reluctantly or not, farmers' attitudes, and the attitudes of male farm workers, began to change as their admiration for the hard work, determination and value of the land girls increased. It is difficult to assess how long lasting this change actually was, and not many people during the 1940s were talking about either feminism or gender issues. As far as most land girls were concerned, they had taken on men's work and they had proved that they were equal to the task. Happily, this was increasingly reflected in statements from farmers themselves.

In May 1941, the *Land Girl* ran an editorial about the publicity that the Land Army was receiving through the press and commented that:

> ...the mountain of Press cuttings leaves one baffled by the variety of vision of people who write to the papers. Some see the Land Army as a solid mass of young Amazons tossing the bull with one hand and throwing hundredweight of sacks around with the other; some have a vision of pale, anaemic females trying to do impossibly heavy tasks...others fear all Land Girls as dangerous and brightly-painted houris, luring the innocent farmer from his happy home...

To counteract the many varying opinions, and the view of a West Kent volunteer that 'The Land Army is the most difficult, unappreciated...of the women's services', and to assure their readers that farmers did appreciate their work, the *Land Girl* published some opinions from farmers who had employed land girls. One came from a farmer in Northumberland, who said:

> They have both proved entirely satisfactory in every way. As you know, I was very doubtful about the wisdom of taking two girls who had had no previous experience. My fears were entirely groundless. They have been quick to learn and have worked hard at all manner of tasks. Not a few of them both dirty and uncongenial. I have nothing but praise for them.

A farmer from Shropshire commented that, 'She is a better worker than any man or woman I have ever had', and a farmer from Staffordshire stated, 'No words of mine can fully express my complete satisfaction and admiration for what they are doing for me here'.

Positive comments appeared elsewhere as well. In August 1941, the *Sussex Express* included comments from Mr Jesse, Director of Agriculture, who praised the work of the land girls, saying:

> ...Although my Land Girl has only been with me a short time, I am able to leave her in sole charge of my dairy calves and cows...
>
> (Worcester farmer, the *Land Girl*, May 1941)

The work they are doing is really excellent, particularly in connection with tractor cultivation, especially considering ...that...they had no previous experience of farming at all. They have picked it up with remarkable skill and it would be almost impossible to improve on their efforts...

Interestingly, when the *Sussex Express and County Herald* reported the views of a disgruntled farmer, in November 1942, who stated that, 'Personally, I would rather be without Land Girls at all, for in my experience they are more bother than they are worth' and went on to say that although he might have been unlucky, in his view 'the Women's Land Army seem to a great extent to be able to please themselves and just turn up or not as they like', there was a furious response. A positive deluge of letters were printed in the *Sussex Express,* not just from land girls defending themselves but also from farmers, farm managers, other workers and the County War Agricultural Committee. It would be wrong to say that all land girls were perfect, or that there were not some unsatisfactory workers, and the rules and regulations of the WLA reflected that possibility, but by far the vast majority fulfilled their commitments and more, as reflected in a letter from one J.C. Robinson, published in the *Sussex Express* on 4 December 1942:

...While there are no doubt a few girls who are a discredit to the Women's Land Army, there are...vast numbers who are the greatest credit to themselves and to this most useful service...A large number of farmers with whom I come in contact speak very highly of the girls they are employing and I fail to see how we should have got through the summer's work without their assistance...

Another who wrote in was William Brown, a farm manager, who expressed his views strongly:

...These girls work all the year round in all weather (despite inadequate clothing), handling all implements connected with arable farming. They work capably, cheerfully, even enthusiastically, and I am prepared to back them against any man of equal experience...To say that girls join the Land

Army to dodge work in the factories and other services seems to me to be quite absurd. No 'dodger' is going into agriculture – probably the hardest work women are tackling at present…

Positive comments were not confined to the farming community; timber merchants also expressed positive views. *Meet the Members* published a tribute from a timber merchant in which he said:

Maybe I've been fortunate, but my girls have proved most satisfactory. At first they did no felling – this was a man's job – and the girls cross-cut the felled trees; this proved monotonous and uninteresting, and provoked a desire to fell and to dispense with the aid of 'mere man'. The early felling was crude (some amusing incidents come to my mind) and the timber suffered from the performance of the girls; but brain and brawn are equally useful in timber felling, and the girls made progress. They accepted advice willingly, and seldom needed the advice repeated. The result is that whilst some have, of necessity, to continue the cross-cutting…others are felling trees of from fifty to two hundred cubic feet…and…the quality of their work compares very favourably with that of the men…

Trade union attitudes, which had been either lukewarm or antagonistic at the beginning of the war, also changed dramatically. In 1944 the *Land Girl* magazine published an article by Mr Arthur Holness of the National Union of Agricultural Workers in which he stated:

The measure of the success of the Women's Land Army is the demand for volunteers. Early in the war it was difficult to place recruits; now there are not enough to go around. Women have, to their credit, magnificent records of successful effort. None have been finer in spirit or achievement than the record of the Women's Land Army…

Mr Holness went on to outline the benefits of joining the union, which many land girls did.

Public Perceptions

By November 1942 an editorial in the *Land Girl* commented that 'Everybody has been saying nice things and there is a general recognition of the value of the Land Army...' but not all land girls would have agreed. Although land girls were generally applauded when they attended rallies or paraded through towns recruiting for more volunteers, and given loud cheers from troops when they went to work, they were rarely in the public eye, and when they did encounter the public, they were often regarded with suspicion, ignorance and dismissiveness. Many land girls felt that the importance of their work was not widely recognized and what they were doing was either taken for granted or not seen as a crucial part of the war effort.

> Girls in the services had many more perks - free travel passes, more leave and plenty of entertainment laid on...nor did they have to give up their clothing coupons in exchange for their uniforms, as we did.
>
> (Pamela McDowell, private papers, with permission)

Phyllis Cole found the local people in Uckfield were welcoming and appreciative because they understood the land girls' work but, on a number of occasions, she met people who knew virtually nothing about the Land Army, and were extremely dismissive. When this happened, she took them to task:

> Some very nasty people said ;You're not doing much during the war', or 'Land Army, well anyone can do that' and I said, 'We're threshing and if we don't thresh, you don't get your bread, you don't get your linseed oil, you don't get beans, you don't get peas.' I said all these different things, and if you talked to them like that, they stopped and listened, and then said, 'Oh, I never realised that'.

She also felt that there was a lot of resentment from women because they were doing a man's job.

The public's attitude towards the Land Army varied. One land girl recorded an occasion when she and five other land girls, having spent the day mucking out cowsheds, boarded the District Line tube at Upminster, only for everyone else in the carriage to walk out. Fortunately, the land girls themselves found it highly amusing but it illustrated the same disdain for those who worked on the land, as the timber workers had encountered when they 'offended' smart diners in a high class hotel. Although most land girls took a surprisingly philosophical and understanding approach to such dismissiveness, there were many who were rightly both hurt and annoyed by snobbish attitudes such as these and the way in which some of the public looked down on land workers.

Cinderella Force

By and large the Forces had respect for the Land Army, and there are many accounts of soldiers assisting land girls, providing them with extra food, making room for them on crowded trains and giving them lifts. But land girls were often regarded as the Cinderella of the women's services because, like Cinderella of the fairy tales, they

> I could not understand why some of the women's services looked down on us. We were doing as much, and sometimes more, for the war effort than they were.
>
> (Grace Wallace, land girl)

were among the most poorly paid and exploited of women wartime workers, and received far less recognition. For Stella Hope, land girls were 'civilians with their rights taken away'.

Land Girls were paid less than women in the munitions factories and did not receive the same wartime benefits as women in the Forces and they were rarely allowed to forget that they were not members of the armed forces. They were forbidden to use forces clubs and could not use canteens that were run for the armed forces at railway stations, despite the fact that they, too, often had to take long and difficult journeys to and from work and home. This could, and did, cause resentment and envy, which happened to Pamela McDowell, when she was refused entry to an ATS canteen in Maidstone. On another occasion land girls, who were returning home during the night after finishing work, went into a YMCA canteen in the early hours of the morning for a cup of tea but were refused service because they were not in the forces. In this case, a soldier standing nearby overheard what had happened, asked how many land girls wanted tea, and on being told there were 26 land girls, went into the canteen and ordered 26 cups of tea, pointing out that the woman there could not refuse to serve him.

Lady Denman and the WLA worked unceasingly to improve benefits for land girls. In 1942 the Women's Land Army Benevolent Fund was launched, to provide financial help for land girls experiencing hardship and, two years later, in 1944, a WLA club was opened in London. But, despite the increasing praise and recognition of achievement that the Ministry of Agriculture, trades unions, and farmers expressed for land girls, they remained second-class citizens when compared with women in other auxiliary services. The situation came to a head as the war neared its end, when it became clear that land girls were not going to receive the same post-war benefits that were to be given to women who had served in the armed forces or civil defence. The argument against this discrimination was long and bitter and eventually led to Lady Denman resigning from the Land Army.

The only opposition you used to get was from the ATS; we used to retaliate and say they were officers' ground-sheets but then you see we were very young.

(Eileen Grabham)

The argument also revealed the extent of prejudice that existed between the women's auxiliary services and members of the Land Army, which was illustrated through a bitter exchange that took place in the columns of the *Land Girl* magazine in 1946. In October 1946 the *Land Girl* printed part of an article by Mrs Aileen Wing, who had served in the WAAF for nearly five years, in which she stated her view that land girls had no idea of how difficult conditions had been in the armed services and that they had only joined the Land Army because 'they were in mortal fear of being conscripted'. In December there were a number of furious replies from land girls, including one lengthy response from D.R. Spearman, who apparently had a sister in the ATS, so felt she did have knowledge of the conditions in the services, and asked:

...Have you ever been sent to a billet where your landlady bitterly resented your presence and was not polite enough to hide it? That also hurts especially if you're by yourself, you know nobody in the village, which is often two or three miles from where you are billeted... As you're a town girl you're inclined to be looked upon as a person of low morals, until at last...you've proved they're wrong...Have you ever been in a cowshed before it's cleaned up, when the cows have been laying in all night and then after milking helped to muck-out – I doubt it...

A Cider Story

One day we went to a farm and the chap said 'I'll pick you up, usual time' and I said 'Well, why have you got to pick us up; it's only at the top of the road, we can walk up'. He laughed and said, 'No, I'll come and pick you up'. We got up there and the man met us at the gate, and the stack was in a huge barn, a big long-sided one and the thresher was put between the two open doors. So we started and it was dusty and of course it was dark in there. So we started about ten or half-past ten and then he said, 'Break girls, come on down you're having a drink. Everybody like cider?' And yes, everybody did like cider; it was beautiful. And then he said, 'We'll have another one in about a couple of hours'. I never did remember finishing that stack. It was just as well we didn't have to walk home because when we came out the chap was standing there and he was laughing and said, 'Look, I took you in the other gate. Look what it says on that gate - Home made cider, very strong!' When you get them like that, it's really good.

(Phyllis Cole)

Chapter 9

Love, Sex and Romance

*O thers fear all Land Girls as dangerous and brightly-painted houris,
luring the innocent farmer from his happy home...*
(The Land Girl, May 1941)

MOST of the women who joined the Land Army were in
their teens or early twenties. It was wartime, most had
left home for the first time, and, as members of the
Women's Land Army, they were not subject to the same rigid
rules and regulations of women in the forces. Once their day's
work was over, land girls were free to do as they pleased.
Soldiers were often billeted nearby and, in theory anyway, there
were plenty of opportunities for love and romance.

Will Lie Anywhere

As their magazine implied, perceived images of land girls
varied from inexperienced young women who just wanted to
cuddle fluffy lambs, through to hefty Amazons and seductive
houris, ready without a moment's notice to entice a farmer, or
his son, away from his tasks for a quick tumble in the hay. There
were farmers' wives and village women who viewed the arrival
of young land girls with foreboding, if not out and out
suspicion, and the image of the seductive land girl was as widespread as the image of the inexperienced recruit washing the
whole cow rather than just its udders.

Women in all the services suffered from sexist perceptions.
Just because they had put themselves into a male role and
donned a uniform, it was assumed that they were making themselves sexually available. The phrase 'Up with the lark and to

bed with a Wren' spoke volumes about how forces women were viewed and the same was true for the land girl. According to Hazel King there were many people, primarily men, who interpreted the initials WLA as 'Will Lay Anywhere', or 'Will Love Anyone' and there were many references to land girls having 'their backs to the land'. Given these attitudes, it is not surprising some parents were reluctant to see their daughters go into the Land Army.

Obviously the combination of youth and war meant that social restrictions and conventions were often cast aside: death was ever present and women took whatever opportunities they could to fall in love and enjoy themselves. Being away from home also meant being away from the ever-watchful eyes of parents. For Pat Parker, who worked with the Timber Corps in Culford, joining was her first experience of complete freedom. Previously, if she went out, she had to be back home by 9 p.m., and her father would wait on the street corner until she returned. Now, in theory anyway, she was free to do as she liked, although in practice, she only went to one dance nearby.

However, the image of the land girl as houri is not only debatable but also insulting and most land girls completely dismiss it. Most of the women interviewed for this book were very critical of the film *The Land Girls*, which appeared in 1998, and included Anna Friel as a man-hungry former hairdresser. During the course of the film, the farmer's son ends up in bed with each of the three land girls billeted on the farm. Many former land girls have been critical and even angry about the way land girls were portrayed in the film. Hazel King was horrified, not because she is, or was, any sort of prude – she claimed she had several boyfriends during the war – but because she felt the portrayal was unjust and inaccurate:

The land girls weren't like that. I was horrified. They all had a go with the farmer's son, well that didn't happen as far as I'm concerned. There were plenty of opportunities but girls who were my age, well you didn't dare. It wasn't like that at all. I was absolutely horrified when I saw it on television. And this Land Army Society that I joined, you should have seen what they wrote about it: the people who ran it [the Society] they said it just wasn't fair.

Obviously, there were casual affairs and some land girls had affairs with married farmers that could disrupt or break up a marriage. Peggy Pearce remembered an occasion when a married farmer became infatuated with her friend. The farmer's wife found out and the land girls promptly moved away from that farm to another posting. But one land girl who joined the Land Army when she was 17, against her parents' wishes, and was sent to North Wales, was emphatic that 'No-one slept around in those days, at least I didn't, perhaps some did but kept very quiet about it.'

Unwanted pregnancies did occur, although many land girls are reluctant to discuss this subject or the topic of affairs, which is hardly surprising. Social mores in the 1940s were strict and women who became pregnant outside marriage faced consider-able difficulties. Some turned to abortions – Pamela McDowell remembered one 'wild and beautiful girl' on a Land Army training course who died during an abortion but establishing detailed information is difficult for a time when abortion was illegal and unmarried mothers could be socially excluded and were expected to give up their babies for adoption. The WLA recognized the possibility and offered some help to unmarried land girls who became pregnant, sending them to hostels and re-employing them once their baby was adopted.

Time Off

Strictly speaking, land girls worked a 48-hour week in winter, and a 50-hour week in summer, although in practice they worked far longer hours. The working week was supposed to be 5½ days, with a half-day off on Saturday afternoons, and all day Sunday. Land girls could take long weekends, if they negotiated it with their employer and made up any working time they might miss.

Once the day's work was over, land girls could please them-selves but what they did with their spare time depended on where they were based, whether they were living in billets or a hostel, on their own or with others. It also depended on what entertainment opportunities existed locally and just how much energy they had after a day's work. Starting around 6 a.m. and not finishing until early evening, meant that most land girls were just too exhausted at the end of the day to do much more than wash and tumble into bed.

Peggy Pearce was in her early twenties when she joined the Land Army. She worked in Gloucester and Surrey and most of the time, shared billets or lived on farms with her friend, Kathleen. They found that there was absolutely nothing to do where they were:

One day a farmer told his two land girls to take the bull down to the cow for siring. The girls set off and were gone for hours. Eventually they came back looking completely dishevelled and as if they had been dragged through a hedge backwards. The farmer asked them what had happened. The land girls replied, 'We couldn't make the cow lie down'.

[Joke told by Bert King, husband of Hazel King]

We didn't have every other weekend off; we worked hours and hours. There wasn't anything to do. We weren't near any soldiers, like a lot of the other girls, not one; every man had gone, except one who was a bit odd. They tried to get a dance up but it was all women; it was fatal. No, we had nothing. Of course there was no television in those days. We had a radio but we were out in the fields and when we came in, the lamp was put on, and what did we do? Half-past eight, we were both asleep on the table. So they used to say 'Come on, you go to bed'. Well we used to go up to bed and I had thick naturally wavy hair, so I didn't have to do anything but Kathleen, poor girl, had to do all this thing with her hair, it had to be all curled, so I would just sit on the bed and I would just fall over; many a time she had to put my legs in, just; but she, poor girl, was ages later than me.

Land girls who lived in hostels had plenty of companionship; in fact some found hostels too rowdy. In the evenings, they entertained themselves, singing and playing the piano or playing board games. Alternatively, depending on what was available in the locality, they might go out. Hostel rules were strict: there was a 10 p.m. curfew and matrons and housekeepers kept a strict eye on when young women returned. Doors were usually locked after 10 p.m. but, not surprisingly, plenty of young women found ways of getting back into the hostel after hours. In her written account, Sheelah Cruttenden described what it was like for her and other land girls living in the WLA hostel at Dumbleton Hall, Worcestershire, where there was plenty going on in the neighbourhood:

> Dumbleton village had no pub but once the local lads and soldiers from the surrounding US army camps got to know the girls better, they were taken further afield to other pubs, darts matches and dances in the surrounding villages. The cinema in either Cheltenham or Evesham were popular venues on Saturday afternoons and I can remember how the girls used to pile on the village bus in such large numbers that I think one bus driver was fined for overcrowding. I recall one particular Saturday in Cheltenham joining the end of a queue outside a theatre only to find Bob Hope with the singer Frances Langford on stage inside.

Sheelah's children, now adults themselves, remember their mother telling them that there were lots of dances and fancy dress parties in the village, which was not far from the hostel. Apparently an Army unit was stationed nearby and some of the young women used to creep out of the hostel to see the soldiers and then creep back in after hours. There was, however, only one record at the hostel:

> They had bands, jitterbug was very popular, village dances, they had one record at the hostel, at Dumbleton and the record was actually called 'Gloomy Tuesday', which was a banned song during the war because it made you feel bad and that was the only one they had.

Boyfriends and Romance

Soldiers were almost everywhere: by 1944 more than 50 per cent of British men between the ages of 19 and 40 were in uniform –

more than 4½ million. And thousands of Canadian, New Zealand and Australian soldiers were also stationed in Britain. Many land girls had boyfriends who were soldiers. Hazel King enjoyed a very active social life when she had time off from ploughing up Romney Marsh:

They were good to us, the troops round here. I suppose they thought they were protecting us – the Wiltshires, the Manchesters, one regiment went and another lot came, just like that. They were in the big houses at the top of Rye Hill. I can remember the Canadians were billeted in St Anthony's and there were some in the High Street, some in the grammar school – the Medical Corps was there. There were troops everywhere. You could just take your pick. You didn't know how many were married; you just had to take their word for it. I had one or two romances. In fact, I used to boast that before I married him [husband Bert], I had 24 boyfriends, but it was harmless. In those days girls didn't go to the pub and drink like they do now. The first time I went in a pub was VE night. There were lots of things going on. There was always a dance or concert in Rye and Saturdays, if we finished at dinner time, we would take ourselves off to Hastings because we had no cinema, it had been bombed. On Saturday nights a travelling cinema came [to Rye] so we could go and see that but we used to go to Hastings, we used to go to the cinema, and have tea. We used to go to a little shop called Moons and we used to have Welsh rarebit and cream buns.

I had several boyfriends during the war. There were so many troops there. You couldn't move for troops. There were all sorts of regiments. It was a case of a broken heart one night and the next night a new boyfriend. It wasn't like it is now; we didn't carry on like they do now. It was more of a friendship thing.

In the event, and despite the many soldiers stationed nearby, Hazel eventually married a farm worker, Bert. She met him one morning and clearly remembers his chat-up line:

I was going down the track and this young man stopped me and he said, 'Your tractor's not running right'. I said, 'It seems all right to me', and he said, 'Well, it isn't. If you'd like to get off, I'll have a look at it for you.' So he fixed the plugs and I got back on and said 'Do you want a lift', so he did and I thought no more about it. And several times he stopped me for a lift, and I thought what a chat-up line.

Bert lived in Appledore, about six miles from Rye: they married in 1946 and, in 2006, celebrated their diamond wedding anniversary.

Helen Dawson also went out with soldiers, and received proposals of marriage:

I was very shy. I went with some soldiers and had three proposals of marriage and I'm so cross, they were lovely, properly done, and my mother cleared things out and she burned them. I was a good girl; they respected me. I was so shy. There was Tom Jones, that was one I went with, he had such blue eyes and of course he went off and you don't know where they are, and he proposed and I was going with someone else then and my Mum said, 'Oh, well' but I'll always regret it...

Hazel later met a man she had seen before who was working on another farm. They married in 1948 and continued working on the land locally.

Pubs, Cinemas and Dances

Social life for land girls was often negligible. The nature of their work meant they were scattered throughout rural districts and the only entertainment might be a local pub, cinema or village hall, and the reality of 'local' could well involve walking for two or three miles.

For Phyllis Cole time off from her threshing duties in Uckfield, usually meant going to the pub or to the vicarage:

We were either going to have a drink at the Barley Mow and giving them a singsong or we were going to church. The vicar there was wonderful: he opened up the house, he invited a lot of young people from the village and we had parties, murder parties over the vicarage and we always went there on Sundays. We went in a group to the Barley Mow and sang loads of things, British songs, war songs, we always finished with Auld Lang Syne; the people around there were wonderful.

To this day, Phyllis continues to re-visit Uckfield where, as a former land girl stationed there, she is always made welcome. She re-married after her time in the Land Army, an upholsterer who had been declared unfit for Army service.

Eileen Hodd, who worked as a land girl in Kent and lived at home, also remembered that entertainment centred on the pub. There were a number of land girls in her village:

> ...they weren't local girls, one girl was from the North, my friend Betty; I think they came from Yorkshire. They were very happy girls. I didn't know them well but you knew them from being in the village; you attended the same sort of social things, which was usually the village pub, well that was the entertainment in those days, and although you weren't drinking, you played darts and shove ha'penny, dominoes and that sort of thing.

Eileen did have boyfriends during the war, and married a soldier, who was billeted in the village. It was a romantic meeting:

> I was on a haystack and he and his mate were having a walk round and he came in the field and we chatted, that sort of thing, and I thought, 'Oh, he's rather nice' and we went down the pub. I went with my friend [Margaret]; and it sort of carried on from there and when he was billeted away we still kept in touch and when he went abroad he wanted me to be his girl and we got engaged and after that, well the war was sort of ended by that time, and he came back and I married him.

142

The romantic story ended tragically however. Eileen and George married in the November after war ended and her husband came to work on the farm with her, but was killed three months later when the tractor overturned. Eileen rarely talks about it today and describes the tragedy as 'all in the life of the Land Army'. She was just 20 when she married and was

pregnant when her husband was killed. Her son was born in 1948 and she went back to live with her mother. She later remarried and she and her husband still live in Rye.

Apart from the occasional dance to go to the only luxury was a hot bath!

(Land Army Reunion, The *Guardian*, 1984)

Margaret Donaldson worked seven days a week and had about one weekend off in three. She made contact with another land girl in the next village and they used to take a bus into Ipswich and go to the cinema, or have a meal on Saturday. There was a village hall nearby, where they went in the winter – during the summer they worked until late – and there was an occasional 'hop', organized by some of the villagers. Margaret used to see soldiers, because she cycled past them, but never saw any in the village and did not go out with any during her time in the Land Army. She 'met a few of the local boys at the village dances and they were quite pleasant, most of them, but I didn't have any boyfriends'. Later, when she was in the ATS she did have a soldier boyfriend who was very keen on her but she 'didn't want to settle down during a war; I was quite determined not to do that'.

Beryl Peacham did not get much time off. During the winter, 'after we'd milked the cows, we used to finish to hear the 6 o'clock news and listen out for any talks that Churchill was going to make and gather round to hear them, in the kitchen'. After that, she went back to the cowsheds on the stroke of 9 p.m. to 'rack them up, offer them buckets of water'. And during the summer, when the hay making was on, she often worked until 10.30 p.m., pulling thistles out of the corn. She remembers the first time she went into a pub:

The first time I ever went to have a drink was with one of the [land] girls. We met in a house in Burwash for that particular day and I sang a song or two. She said what about going to The Bear to have a drink one evening. So we went down there and she said 'What are you going to drink?' and I said 'I don't know', thinking madly what to drink and I suddenly thought of brown ale because I think Dad had one once. And she thought maybe she would have a brown ale and then she changed her mind and we went in The Bear.

Land girls themselves provided entertainment, putting on performances and shows for village people. Beryl Peacham commented on one performance they organized in Burwash: '…we put on a variety show, there was a wonderful girl who sang; we performed to the village people in Burwash in the village hall. I wore my breeches'. In 1944 the *Sussex Express* printed rave reviews of an ambitious performance at Battle at which a variety of land girls had sung popular songs from opera, and recited poetry.

Dances were sometimes organized that might be held in a village or at an army camp and land girls, if time allowed, piled onto lorries or cycled to the hop. Some wore civilian clothes but most chose to wear their Land Army uniform, although one land girl thought that dancing in breeches with soldiers looked extremely funny. Quite a number of land girls encountered prejudice at dances, particularly from women in other services. One land girl remembers being completely 'ostracized' by service women who refused to talk to land girls and Pat Parker who worked in the Timber Corps described one village dance when the call came for a special Land Army Paul Jones, women of the Timber Corps who stepped into the middle of the dance floor were quite obviously not welcome. Local people, too, were not always welcoming. One land girl, Madge Humphries, who was one of 32 Yorkshire land girls, stationed in a village called Wrangle, about 7 miles from Boston, Lincolnshire remembered that: 'The old people in the village were very nice to us but the young girls were spiteful towards us. We weren't welcome in the village pub.'

Sometimes American GIs were stationed nearby, and they organized dances and invited land girls. Recollections of

Americans vary but there are often references to the food on American bases, which was better and more plentiful than the normal run of wartime rations in Britain, as Joan Markby commented:

> When the Americans came, we had the American air force dance bands, who played at dances. The Americans were really super; there was no problem. You could walk about at night, not like now, and they were very nice and they gave us tins of SPAM.

Blanche Lucas was another former land girl who remembered the American soldiers with fondness:

> There was a great big hall over the milk factory, down in Maiden Newton, we walked or cycled down there (3½ miles), I can't think how we did it now, it was lovely dances when the Americans were there with the band, we did have other troops there before, but of course this band came over and it was absolutely wonderful, just like Glen Miller, so we were very thrilled at that and then there was a Thanksgiving lunch, which I was lucky enough to go to. I got picked up in a jeep and then there was turkey and pumpkin pie and that was lovely when you were hungry.

American soldiers had a reputation for 'getting girls in trouble' but women interviewed for this book thought very highly of them. Some land girls fell in love with American GIs, although only a few married American soldiers, who were very exotic to British eyes. A few land girls encountered black GIs; for many this was the first time they had ever seen a black person, but it was usually from a distance because a strict colour bar operated in the American forces.

Going Home

Those who could, tried to get back to see their families as often as possible. Blanche Lucas, who worked in Brightling, Sussex, remembered having half a day off every week and one weekend a month; she used to cycle home to Ashburnham, which was about five or six miles away. Sheelah Cruttenden went home regularly at weekends but it was too far to cycle so she hitched lifts, always wearing her uniform:

Wearing my uniform and always with a friend, I would hitch a lift from the main road, my first lift ever being in the back of a lorry carrying bottles of blood rattling in crates! Both train and bus were used for the return journey to the hostel.

The WLA provided free travel passes for those who lived more than 20 miles away and who had completed six months' continuous employment but rural transport, never frequent at the best of times, was, like everything else, disrupted by war. Sometimes Phyllis Cole went home on Friday nights to visit her mother in Hastings but public transport was unreliable and not always available:

They gave us a pass to get there so we went by train to Lewes, and then from Lewes we got a bus but they changed all the schedules and buses didn't always go that far, we used to walk to or from the station and get the bus. People were so kind; they'd stop and say, 'Where are you going girls? Down to the station? We'll take you to the station.' They were wonderful.

Eileen Grabham, whose home was in London while she worked in Rye, remembered that when she was doing fieldwork:

We had every weekend off but I couldn't always afford to go home. There was only about one bus a week to Ashford from New Church. We used to go to Ashford and wander around.

Marriage

Quite a number of land girls got married during the war, and many of the weddings were reported in the local press. With clothes rationing, women either made their own dresses out of whatever material was available, or borrowed wedding dresses. When one of their number got married, other land girls stood outside the church as a guard of honour, using their pitchforks to make an arch.

Barbara Giles, 85, joined the Land Army when she was 17 and worked in Sussex: 'I got married when I was in the Land Army and I had all the land girls outside the church. I had a white wedding and all the land girls came. I didn't marry a farmer, quite a lot of land girls did but I married a chap who worked on the railways.' Barbara became pregnant and when recruitment started again for the Land Army in 1945, she was asked to go back: 'They came to the door of the farm but I was about seven months pregnant, so he said "What I've come for, I didn't need to come", so I couldn't really go back. I would have gone back if I could. I loved it there.'

Quite a number of land girls married farmers' sons or farm workers, and continued working on the land until they became pregnant.

Keeping Up Appearances

Despite Vita Sackville-West's references to land girls in 'mouse-like obscurity', when they went out for the day or in the evening, they were visible. New clothes were hard to come by and land girls, like women throughout wartime Britain, had to 'make do and mend'. Some wore civilian clothes when they went out but many chose to wear their uniforms, saving elements such as the breeches, overcoat and thick socks for 'best'. Uniforms had to be worn for any official engagements or rallies and many were also expected to go home in their uniform, so that parents or other relatives could show them off. Rose Hignett remembered: 'If I visited my uncle or aunt, I didn't dare not go in uniform and he'd [my uncle] take me round all the pubs and show me off.'

Land girls were constantly reminded that they had a responsibility to uphold the good name of the Land Army; they represented an important national service and their behaviour reflected on the organization. Keeping up appearances, particularly when it came to wearing uniform, was a constant theme. It was such an important topic that, in April 1942, Margaret Pyke dedicated her *Land Girl* editorial to the question of uniformity and the need to wear the uniform properly. Starting the article with a quote from someone who had said that there was no doubt that 'the Land Army has the most attractive uniform of all the Women's Services', the editorial went on to stress the need for 'uniformity', saying:

> ...Come out as gay or as shabby or as Bohemian as you like in civilian clothes but don't try to express your personality in your uniform...a volunteer seen in the streets of a large town (this is a true story) wearing a hat cocked on one side and tied on with red ribbon in a large bow under her chin, red tie and fancy shoes with otherwise correct uniform, makes passers-by gaze at her with a wild surmise as to whether it is she or the Land Army which has gone crackers...

You couldn't wear a dress on the tractor. I do remember in the mornings, being girlies, all the time we were in the war we wore a flower in our hair.

(Hazel King, tractor driver)

Wearing the hat correctly was of particular concern. In an early issue (August 1940), the *Land Girl* ran a series of four photographs, showing how the hat should be worn: forward and slightly to one side, not right back on the head. Vita Sackville-West also picked up the same theme, stating that:

> ...in the streets you do not see them [land girls] at their best. They are dressed up then, for their outing, and there is surely no one who can do more extraordinary things with a uniform than the Land-girl who has really put her mind to it...It is a source of despair to the poor Land Army official, who knows better than anybody how well these girls deserve to be taken seriously, and who is compelled to watch *some* of them exposing themselves to a thoughtless ridicule...

Having discussed topics such as the way land girls wore their 'breeches', Vita Sackville-West went on to the ever important topic of the hat:

> ...And as for the things some of them do with their hats and their hair...The Land-girl is given a brown slouch hat, intended to be worn straight over reasonably controlled

hair. She could look as romantic as a cowboy in it if she liked; and indeed...it is not unlike the hats affected by...Tom Mix...The trouble is that she forgets all about the Tom and remembers only the Mix... You cannot look fashionable in uniform... She builds her hair up in such a way that no hat could possibly be expected to stay in place, adds a bootlace to her hat, and uses it as a chin strap...

To the exasperation of the WLA officials, many land girls did tinker with their uniform to try and make it a bit more fashionable although not always with great success. Eileen Grabham, 'used to wear it [hat] with the cord like a cowboy. How we got away with it, I don't know. We were supposed to wear it like a po, but we dented it in. It's difficult to imagine now isn't it?'

Land girls also tinkered with their working clothes. Some former land girls remember being reprimanded for rolling up their trousers to make them into shorts during the hot weather, which was cooler and also meant the chance of getting tanned legs, useful at a time when silk stockings were virtually unknown, so that young women stained their legs with tea and drew a line up the back of the leg to imitate stocking seams.

Audrey Blythe, who was based at Brenzett Hostel in Kent, remembered one occasion when she and her friends prepared for an evening out:

We used to have dungarees and those aertex shirts. We bleached them overnight, bleached them to a lovely cream colour and then we wore them back to front, so it was like a roll collar with our new dungarees and we were going to hitchhike into Deal, five miles. This guy stopped with a sports car and gave all five of us a life and he said, 'Girls, have you just knocked off work?' We were really insulted; we thought we were the cat's whiskers.

Chapter 10

End of War

I don't know why we weren't recognized. Lady Denman was furious about it.

(Barbara Giles)

BY MID-1944, the tide of war was beginning to turn and there was increasing optimism that the Allies would be victorious. The long war was taking its toll: soldiers and civilian war workers alike were weary but it was a matter of gritting teeth and carrying on. Margaret Pyke summed up the situation in her editorial in the *Land Girl* in January 1945, when she wrote:

> The sixth winter of the war is perhaps the most difficult and trying time of all the difficult and trying times which the British nation has had to endure since the summer of 1939. Most of us are overtired and overworked... None of us questions the necessity of putting up with these things because we know it is the only way to win the war...

The Need Continues

Margaret Pyke's comments were pertinent because, by this time, the Government had realized the Land Army was going to be needed for quite some while. Once war was over, it would take time for soldiers to be demobilized and POWs would be repatriated, leaving a significant gap in the agricultural labour force. Consequently, the Government decided that a further 30,000 land girls were needed to fill this gap, and recruitment for the Land Army, which had been closed in 1943, started up again.

Local and national press ran appeals for more land girls, as did the pages of the *Land Girl* magazine, which began a feature welcoming new recruits.

Regional and local newspapers also put out appeals, including the *Sussex Express and County Herald* which, in December 1944, reported on a Christmas rally of land girls from all over East Sussex that was held at the De La Warr Pavilion, Bexhill. County chairman, Countess de la Warr, had addressed the assembled land girls, and was quoted as saying: '...At the moment the Land Army has got to go full steam ahead. The war isn't won and the food situation is just as bad as it was.' Concerning the Land Army's future, she went on to say: 'We asked the Minister of Agriculture and all he could tell us was the food situation is going to be very bad... Therefore the Land Army has got to go on for at least two years after the war.' In the event, the Land Army would carry on working for another five years after the war, until 1950.

By now the Land Army had more than proved its worth: as early as 1943 it had helped British farming achieve all the Government's targets and by early that year its work had ensured that food imports had dropped to just half a million tons, the lowest since the start of war. Land Army workers had shown critics not only that they could they do the work, but also that productivity levels had increased. Sceptics had been proved wrong and the Land Army had won the support of virtually everyone in the farming community as well as the trade unions, who had gained land army members.

When I eventually leave the Land Army, my gratuity will go with me, not in the form of money granted by the Government, but rather something no money can buy, robust health, a contented mind and a feeling of a job well and truly done.

(S. Pearse, Devon, the *Land Girl* May 1946)

As a result, the new recruits – and women responded to the appeals for more workers in great numbers – were volunteering into a very different atmosphere from that in 1939. However, behind the scenes all was not well and it soon became clear that although the farming community now valued the land girls, there were some in the Government who did not and the Land Army's great achievements were not going to be officially recognized.

Shabby Treatment

Lady Denman had battled tirelessly to improve conditions for land girls and to achieve a more equal status for them in relation to other services. She had achieved a great deal, including paid holidays, improved wages and access, in principle, to some facilities used by other services. But land girls never enjoyed equal status with women in the auxiliary forces and this became increasingly clear as the end of the war approached. Early signs dated back to 1942 when an official from the Ministry of Agriculture wrote to Lady Denman telling her that he had been unable to persuade the Government to include land girls in proposals for post-war retraining and education. Lady Denman protested, saying she found it strange 'that a civilian nurse should be eligible for training as a veterinary surgeon but that a member of the Women's Land Army should be debarred from this advantage'. The discrimination, however, was to get worse.

In 1944 the Government passed the Reinstatement in Civil Employment Act, which made provision for forces men and women to be reinstated in civilian employment. The Act excluded members of the Land Army, who were to be given no

When I was demobbed in 1945 I had to return all my uniform, even socks which had been darned. In return for my services, I was allowed to keep my overcoat, and was given 10 clothing coupons. I know it is not always possible to mention everyone who helped in the war. I was told that, if you were conscripted or volunteered to wear a uniform and the King's crown on your badge, you belonged to one of the services. We had discipline, rules and punishment, just the same as the ATS, WAAF and WRENS. We had to go where we were told. For many years on Remembrance Sunday, we have not been asked to be represented. The question is, why not? Do we not deserve to be recognized with pride and honour? Why were we forgotten so easily after we were no longer needed? We were proud then to wear our uniform and serve our country.

(Grace Wallace, WLA Lancashire)

post-war help or gratuities. Lady Denman challenged this, pointing out that land girls had given up good jobs to help their country and that the decision was unjust, citing the case of a land girl whose job had been taken by a young woman who had subsequently joined another branch of the women's services: 'It seems most unfair that the second girl should have a prior claim to reinstatement.' Lady Denman also lobbied for land girls to receive the same post-war clothing coupons and grants that were to be offered to women in the services but without any success.

By autumn 1944 it was clear that Robert Hudson, Minister of Agriculture and a good friend to the Land Army, could not win any concessions and that the War Cabinet had decided land girls would be excluded from all post-war benefits. Their argument was simple: land girls were civilian workers and, if the Government made benefits available to them, they would also have to make benefits available to munitions and other industrial war workers. Lady Denman's argument was that land girls were quite different from industrial workers: they belonged to an officially designated 'Army', wore state-supplied uniform and had accepted a pledge of mobile service, but it was not accepted. It was a particularly mean and ironic decision because it was made just as the Government was insisting on the need for more land girls.

Many people, including former land girls, have wondered why this decision was made. Nicole Tyrer in her excellent book, *They Fought in the Fields*, has suggested that the decision, which was primarily made by Winston Churchill and Ernest Bevin, might have been personal – there was little love lost between Churchill, Bevin and Lady Denman. It may have been based on a deep misogyny – Churchill, after all, was no supporter of votes for women in the early years of the Twentieth Century – or it may have reflected the lack of regard for agricultural workers. Either way, it was a very shabby way to treat the women who had worked so hard on the land producing the nation's food.

Some of the women interviewed for this book, although many are now well into their 80s, are still angered or hurt by the decision, even though time has blunted the emotions, and many do not understand why it happened. For Rose Hignett, 83, the lack of recognition was 'disgusting...we kept them going with the food, didn't we?' and her view was echoed by many. Generous to a fault, some former land girls felt it might have been because they did not face the same dangers as other women. Eileen Grabham, for instance, was less worried about the lack of recognition because:

> I feel there were some people who had far more dangerous jobs than we did, those people who were in intelligence and who were dropped behind enemy lines and could be tortured. It never worried me [lack of recognition] but I know it does a lot of girls.

Eileen Hodd correctly noticed that land girls were not the only ones who were excluded:

> I don't think the Land Army did [get the recognition it deserved] because I suppose you were doing the sort of home work that nobody recognized. It was just an ordinary job. I suppose the factory workers never got recognized did they? I mean the ammunition and the plane workers; they never really got recognized did they? It must have been tough for them.

Lady Denman Resigns

Lady Denman finally accepted that she could not win the same post-war benefits for land girls as for forces women and men, but then Ernest Bevin announced that resettlement grants of £150 would be given to Civil Defence and auxiliary workers but not land girls. For Lady Denman this was the last straw and she decided she had no option but to resign. She warned Robert Hudson of her intention and, on 16 February 1945, having alerted the press, she sent him a letter of resignation:

> ...I write with regret to notify you of the decision foreshadowed...and to tender you my resignation from the Office of Honorary Director of the Women's Land Army for England and Wales. The Land Army is a uniformed service recruited

on a national basis by a Government Department and the work which its members have undertaken, often at considerable financial sacrifice, is in my view as arduous and exacting as any branch of women's war work and of as great importance to this country. Yet they have been refused post-war benefits and privileges accorded to such other uniformed and nationally organized services as the W.R.N.S., the A.T.S., the W.A.A.F., the Civil Nursing Reserve, the Police Auxiliaries and the Civil Defence Services.

The position is a serious one for Land Army members who will have as great a need as those in other services of Government assistance in the problems of re-settlement. As you know, I have protested against the omission of the Land Army from various Government schemes and also against the decision, now announced, that capital grants to assist in re-starting business enterprises will be available after the war to men and women who have served whole time in the Forces, the Merchant Navy or the Civil Defence Services but not to members of the Women's Land Army. It is this latest decision which has led me to feel that I must resign my present appointment and that I can no longer appear to be responsible for a policy with which I do not concur...

...I have held the view that one of my chief functions has been to get a square deal for members of the Land Army and I have felt personal responsibility for policy affecting their welfare. The latest decision of the Government therefore made me decide that my position had become untenable...

Lady Denman stepped down from her position as Honorary Director and Mrs Inez Jenkins took over the reins.

We weren't counted and the merchant navy weren't counted at all in the parades, I never could understand it. There we were; we'd got a uniform, we did our best for the country, we worked very hard indeed and mostly without moaning. Well, I was very proud to be one of them, I'm still proud; there were even one or two who got killed. After so many years and then not so long ago, all these reunions started, like the one at Brenzett.

(Beryl Peacham)

In March 1945, the *Land Girl* editorial reported on Lady Denman's resignation; Margaret Pyke described it as a 'shattering blow to all those who have been connected with the Land Army during nearly six years of honourable history'. The following month, the *Land Girl* published a farewell message from Lady Denman, in which she explained her reasons for resigning and expressed her sadness. She urged the organization to continue with its essential work, and thanked the Land Army members for their support:

I have felt it a great honour to be Honorary Director of the Women's Land Army which through dark and dangerous days has helped to deprive Hitler of his weapon of starvation. England owes much to you members of the Land Army for what you have done and you will realize that the people of this country appreciate the service you have given.

I am indeed sad to say goodbye to you, but I hope that my resignation may draw public attention, including the attention of the House of Commons to the privileges and awards given to the Forces and Civil Defence which are not extending to you.

I know that many of those working in the Land Army organization would like to add their protest to mine, but I hope that Chairmen, Members of County Committees, County Secretaries and their staffs and Local Representatives will feel able to stay in their posts... The need for your work is as great now as it has always been, the years after the war will be lean years and a time of want and starvation in many parts of Europe. You experienced workers will have the satisfaction of knowing that in working for agriculture you are helping of stave off the disaster of an under-fed population...

Lady Denman went on to tell members of the Land Army that the Ministry of Agriculture was planning training courses for those who wanted to stay on the land – which many women did – and to hope that those who remained on the land would eventually manage their own farms and gardens. She also expressed her wish that the links made between town and country would survive beyond the war and that women who went back to the towns would not forget the country, saying that they knew 'the avoidable disadvantages under which country people live' and should do whatever they could to make 'townsfolk' understand them.

Public Outcry

Lady Denman's resignation became public on 17 February 1945 and was widely covered in the national and regional press, which was highly critical of the War Cabinet's decision and sympathetic towards the Land Army. For the first time the discrimination experienced by the Land Army had become front page news and the public and the farming community took the opportunity to express their displeasure.

National newspapers such as *The Times* and the *Manchester Guardian* ran editorials deploring the decision and calling on the Government to change its mind, as did the regional press. On 23 February, 1945 the *Sussex Express and County Herald*, in its regular feature 'Topics of the Week' carried a piece entitled 'Fair Play for WLA', in which it said that one good result of Lady Denman's resignation 'is to arouse public feeling with regard to the official treatment of this important national service', and went on to deplore the fact that the WLA's uniformed service, 'recruited on a national basis by the Government, has always been treated as the Cinderella of the women's war services…This official aloofness has sometimes been carried so far that the Women's Land Army has seemed to have no recognized status and a work which should have ranked first in national needs, has almost been relegated to the background…'

The East Sussex County Chairman, Mrs Madge Brooke wrote a letter to the paper in support of Lady Denman, telling readers that a delegation of chairmen had called on the Ministry of Agriculture and written to the National Farmers Union (NFU), and that local MPs had tabled motions in the House of Commons calling for the WLA to be recognized and for the matter to be debated in the House. In March 1945 the paper reported that the East Sussex County Executive of the NFU had decided, by an overwhelming majority, to support the motion to grant members of the Land Army proper facilities for training and rehabilitation, clothing coupons, and the right to retain their badges. That month the paper featured a dramatic picture of land girls working in the fields entitled 'They've earned a Gratuity' with an accompanying caption stating:

It's hard, dirty, thirsty work. Girls of the Women's Land Army took up this and other agricultural work to help the country in its hour of need and they've earned practical recognition.

The same sentiments were echoed up and down the country from individual farmers, representatives of the National Farmers' Union and the Agricultural Farm Workers Union. The Queen also offered to give whatever help she could.

Small Concessions

Members of Parliament took up the land girls' cause, including Labour MP Edith Summerskill, a bitter critic of Winston Churchill. Nearly 200 MPs from all parties signed motions protesting the Government's decision to exclude land girls from post-war benefits being given to other services and the issue was hotly debated in Parliament. Churchill was asked to receive a deputation of MPs but he and Bevin refused to budge from their decision.

Ultimately, given the strength of feeling in the country and in Parliament, some minor concessions were made in May 1945. Some state help would be made available for land girls who wanted to do further training in agriculture or in other work, equivalent to that being offered to Civil Defence and auxiliary war workers. The Government undertook to pay £150,000 to the Land Army Benevolent Fund, and it was decided that when land girls left the Land Army they could keep their greatcoats, provided these were dyed blue, and their shoes.

Strikes and Protests

The concessions were petty and small-minded and it is extraordinary how philosophically many land girls received the decision. Some, however, were extremely angry. One wrote saying:

> I joined in June 1939. I have lost my pre-war office job (they sacked me when I volunteered) and as far as the Government is concerned my future would be completely blank – my sole souvenir of five and a half long years' loyal service a rather battered scarlet armband – not even a discharge badge.

Other land girls were angry enough to take direct action. During the war, quite a few had joined the Agricultural Workers Union. They set up a fighting fund, formed a committee, and drafted a National Charter of demands, including more clothing coupons, 2/- a week gratuity, and more money to be paid into the Land Army Benevolent Fund. A number of land girls demonstrated in London and lobbied the Minister of Agriculture and Winston Churchill, without success. According to *Time* magazine, some 300 land girls from as far as Wales, Yorkshire and Lancashire descended on London, met at Caxton Hall, and demonstrated with placards, pointing out the inequalities between women in the ATS and those in the Land Army: their slogan – 'Give us a square deal, and we'll give you a square meal.'

There were also a number of strikes. On 14 April 1945 the *Gloucestershire Echo* reported that about 150 land army girls in North Gloucestershire had called a one-day strike as a protest against the non-granting of gratuities by the Government. Land girls came into Cheltenham from WLA hostels at Dumbleton Hall, Southam Priory, Berkeley, Tetbury and Oaklands, and paraded through the streets in their uniforms. One of their number was quoted as saying, 'It is only a one-day strike to show our disgust at the unfairness of the Government's attitude. We have no intention of shirking our duties, and will resume these tomorrow.' Apparently passers by were extremely sympathetic. Union and WLA officials visited the hostels and the land girls returned to work the following day. Sheelagh Cruttenden was stationed at Dumbleton Hall: according to her children, she actually took part in the strike – in fact she appears in a photograph of the event which appeared in the *Gloucestershire Echo* –

and told them that those who did so were docked a day's pay. Strikes also took place in Buckinghamshire, Suffolk and Essex.

Land Army officials frowned on this sort of direct action, even if they understood the reasons for it. In her *Land Girl* editorial of April 1945, Margaret Pyke stated that Lady Denman's resignation had done all that was needed to rouse public sympathy and that although there were many who, given the Government's intransigence, might want to throw down their spades and ploughs, it was not be recommended. Appealing to the good name of the WLA, she wrote:

> ...If the rest of us went, the Government would not suffer but the country would...The high place the WLA has won in the opinion of the people of Britain has been demonstrated by the public sympathy for its cause...Neither resentment nor the elation of victory must tempt members of the Land Army to do anything which will lower their reputation or imperil the production of food for lack of which even one man, woman or child might starve...

Most land girls opposed the use of direct action and said so. In May 1945 one wrote to the *Land Girl* criticizing those girls who had recently gone on strike, saying that 'the action did more harm than good'.

Victory Parades and Pieces of Paper

In May 1945 Germany surrendered and the war in Europe ended. Three months later, in August, Japan surrendered and the Second World War finally came to an end after six long years. The process of demobilization got underway, wartime organizations were closed down and gradually wartime workers were shifted back into civilian occupations or, in the case of women, often encouraged to return to the home. But the Land Army carried on.

Some land girls had already left, particularly those who had married during the war and become pregnant but, by 1945, there were still 54,000 working on the land and new recruits were joining. When the war ended all land girls received an official letter telling them they were now free to leave if they wished, but thousands decided to remain. Those who left received a brief letter, signed by the Queen, thanking them for their service and wishing them well. Over time the letters became more personal but mistakes were sometimes made. Sheelah Cruttenden, who always believed her Land Army days were among the happiest days of her life, was rather disappointed to find that her name had been misspelled and some of her service left out:

> ...I was given a certificate to commemorate my contribution to the war effort, signed by Queen Elizabeth (the Queen Mother) Unfortunately I had to alter the spelling of my name and also the years of service did not include those from 1947 to 1949 in Sussex...

Sheelah's children remember that their mother often referred to the fact that:

> ...her certificate hadn't given her recognition for the last three years, because it was only for 1942-1946, so that was the first thing she was cross about and they spelled her name wrong; she was really cross about that and I think she was cross about no gratuity. We always said to her that she should have got a medal. She should have got those two that Dad got. She just had her badge. She was upset and we were upset for her. They got a raw deal. They weren't on the frontline so maybe that's why.

Others felt much the same way: a greatcoat, pair of shoes and a certificate from the Queen were hardly adequate ways of expressing thanks for their work. Even so, few land girls were left in any doubt that the Queen – and the public – did appreciate their invaluable contribution to the war effort. On 7 December 1945 the Queen threw a party at Mansion House for the Land Army and presented golden armlets to 235 members who were early recruits and had worked continuously throughout the war. Her speech was printed in the January 1946 issue of the *Land Girl*:

> ...I wish to express my thanks to you and to all other Land

Army members for what you have done and to tell you how deeply I share in the admiration which the whole Country feels for your achievements.

...You came in those distant days six years ago, with your great gifts of youth and strength and with high purpose, to serve your Country in her hour of need, and never have British women and girls shown more capacity or more pluck. On the farms and in the fields, forests and gardens, you took your place in the Battle of Freedom, and through your endurance and your toil you supplied the needs of this Island and sustained the life of the nation.

I realize how hard your work has often been, how lonely sometimes, far from home and family, in strange and unfamiliar surroundings and conditions, but your courage, your resourcefulness and your almost unfailing cheerfulness carried you through every difficulty.

You have gained a great reputation by your skill and your selfless service and, as your Patron, I am indeed proud and I rejoice with you, and with your devoted officers, that the Land Army should have won for itself so fair a name and should so truly deserve it...

Six months later, in June 1946, the British public also showed its appreciation of the Land Army when land girls and timber workers marched with others on a huge Victory Parade through London. The *Land Girl* covered the victory celebrations in great detail and the editorial reported that the massive reception the Land Army received was 'almost overwhelming to the volunteers who took part in it', going on to state that there was a 'special outburst of applause' for the 'green jerseys'. According to Margaret Pyke, it was 'the first chance the nation has had to show what it thinks of the W.L.A. and it expressed its opinion in no uncertain voice (even a police horse neighed its salute)...' One land girl who had taken part in the parade wrote:

One by one each group of the Civilian Contingent moved forward, then came our signal – we were really beginning. As we passed through the thousands of waiting soldiers, cheer after cheer rang out for the Land Army. We landed an extra special cheer from the Brigade of Guards and the Infantrymen. As we passed the Life Guards Band, the C.O. saluted us and said, 'Well done-Good Girls'. By now we were in sight of Marble Arch. Never have I seen so many people – at every window – on every building – no matter where you looked, there were people. We had a terrific reception – cheer after cheer went up for the Land Girls – on two occasions women broke through the police and tried to shake hands with some of us.

Sadly, however, this was almost the last time that the Land Army received such a public acknowledgement. There were subsequent parades but they passed almost unnoticed, and to the immense disappointment of many former land girls, the WLA was not invited to the march past at the Cenotaph on Remembrance Sunday until more than 50 years later.

Post-War Options

From 1945 land girls had the choice of returning to civilian life, or remaining in the Land Army. Many married during the war, or shortly afterwards, and, if possible, continued working on the land, sometimes with their husbands. Once pregnant, however, married women had to leave the land, although some returned to it in a civilian capacity when their children were old enough. Many were very reluctant to leave and even after the Land Army was disbanded, some 5,000 women remained on the land in one capacity or another.

Those who chose to leave had various options, some of which were presented to them through the pages of the *Land Girl*. From August 1945 the magazine ran a series of articles on possible choices for de-mobbed land girls stating that 'women are needed as teachers, librarians, workers in the book trade, journalists and writers...' in what was described as the 'battle of education'. The Government was setting up the post-war Welfare State to overcome what William Beveridge had described as the 'five giants' of 'Want, Disease, Ignorance, Squalor and Idleness' and the land girls were encouraged to play their part in overcoming these. It was suggested that they could go into nursing and teaching but, above all, articles in the magazine stressed the importance of the housewife, stating that: 'The woman who is building a home now, who is deciding to bring up children, is the guardian of the peace of the world…there is no career that can compare with this one.' It was a message that was being sent out to all women at the end of the war, to get them back into the home and release waged work for men. As happened after the First World War, many women did return to the home but not in the same way, or for as long. War work had given women confidence and independence; they had proved that they could manage their own lives and many found that the return to domesticity was difficult. Within twenty or so years, women would be demanding a fuller and more equal role in society.

The Land Army Winds Down

A surprising number of women chose to remain in the Land Army and there were also new recruits. Initially there was a great deal of work for them to do; rationing not only continued but also intensified after the war for a few years and the first winter after the war was a bitter one. But, slowly, the Land Army wound down. The Women's Timber Corps was disbanded in August 1946 and the *Land Girl* magazine ceased publication in March 1947, with a final editorial that reiterated how the magazine had started when a young Land Army 'had just begun to show a rather sceptical world what it could do' and described how proud the magazine had been to publicize the triumphs of the WLA, saying that some of these had been spectacular 'like the hundreds of volunteers who ploughed the fields (but did *not* scatter) in the midst of the Battle of Britain…' A free magazine, *Land Army News*. replaced it.

As time went on there was less work for land girls to do, and their numbers dwindled. One of their final achievements was helping to eradicate the Colorado Beetle, a dreadful pest. Land girls were sent in teams with DDT to spray the fields. Looking back, Stella Hope remembered that: '…one of the cushiest jobs I had was six weeks on what was called the Colorado Beetle Job. This involved going round the countryside of north Kent, plotting any field over half an acre that had potatoes in case of an infestation of Colorado Beetle'.

In 1948 the Land Army county committees, which Vita Sackville-West had described as the 'the ends of the arteries' of the Land Army, were dissolved and, in October 1949, it was announced that the Land Army would be wound up the following year. Many land girls were dismayed by the news and even the National Farmers' Union protested against the decision, but, on 21 October 1950, the Land Army, which by then numbered about 8,000 land girls, was finally stood down. Five hundred land girls marched past Buckingham Palace in their final stand-down parade and the Queen made a speech, once again thanking them for their work. Lady Denman was awarded the Grand Cross of the British Empire.

A Forgotten Army Recognized

The Land Army's achievements were extraordinary: against all odds and having to overcome enormous prejudice at the outset, more than 80,000 women, most of them very young, in their teens or early twenties, and at least one third of them from towns and cities, had taken on what was previously considered to be an exclusively male world, had learned new and demanding skills and had helped to keep Britain fed through six long years of war. Civilians in Germany and many of the occupied countries, notably Holland, had starved, but in Britain, although stringent rationing could not be avoided, starvation was never a possibility. Inexperienced young women from towns and cities had adapted to strange and unfamiliar conditions and had taken on the most strenuous and possibly least regarded of all work, and proved that they were capable of doing whatever was asked of them from thistle dodging to tractor driving and rat killing. During the process, they had stimulated British farming and made significant links between town and country.

Despite their achievements, many former land girls consider that they were the 'forgotten army'. The WLA is one of the least talked about women's war services, except among themselves, and it was not until 1995 that the Land Army re-emerged into

I wanted to do that [march past the Cenotaph]; I would have loved to have done that. I've always said to my husband 'Look at that, no Land Army'. We were overlooked. Why? Because they thought we were doing perhaps an unnecessary job. We were helping the farmers, we were making sure they got all the things, the peas, the beans, and it had all got to be cleaned away each year, I had a good mind to write to someone but I didn't know who to write to. It was the lack of recognition that I thought was so awful, that's why I always call it the forgotten army.

(Phyllis Cole)

the public eye, when some 80 former land girls, most of them well into their 70s marched in London to celebrate the 50th anniversary of VJ-Day. Since then there has been a growing interest in the WLA, with the publication of various books, oral histories and websites. Some of the women interviewed for this book, such as Phyllis Cole and Blanche Lucas, have given talks about their experiences to local societies and others have contributed to recorded archives and CDs. Recognition has come late and it was not until 2000 that the WLA was finally invited to the Remembrance Day march past at London's Cenotaph. As Joan Markby has said:

I think it was good we were recognized at last; we were doing a man's job, which was hard work. We're still going on but we can't get about much. There won't be anyone to come soon.

A few months after this comment, in December 2007, the British government finally announced that a special badge was to be awarded to surviving members of the WLA in recognition of their service during the Second World War.

Chapter 11

Reflections

I absorb with greed my heritage, content
That I lived this hour. Be this my gratuity.
(Joyce Oehring, *Poems of the Land Army*)

IT IS possible that one of the reasons the Land Army received such little recognition is because those who work in farming are still undervalued and that farming itself is of little interest to most people, particularly those who live in towns who talk romantically of the country but have little understanding of the difficulties involved in trying to earn a living from the land. There is still a big divide between town and country and few people who live in towns really appreciate the difficulties that the farming community faces. At the beginning of the war, many farmers, somewhat wearily, believed that the Government's interest in their lives was only caused by a national emergency and most resented the fact that untrained young women were being foisted onto them. As the war progressed, however, it does seem as if a great understanding and sympathy developed between the farming community and the army of young women who adapted to life on the land and proved their work to farmers and villagers throughout Britain.

A Special Place

Despite the lack of official recognition, there is little doubt that being in the Land Army or the Timber Corps was an overwhelmingly positive experience for the young women who volunteered to work on the land, and one that they have never forgotten. Most of the women interviewed for this book say that being in the Land Army was one of the happiest and most rewarding experiences of their lives and had it not been for the end of the war or marriage, they would have continued doing the work for much longer. They gained independence, learned skills that they would never have acquired otherwise and proved to themselves, irrespective of others, that they were capable of tackling work previously considered only appropriate for men. Those who came from the towns also gained an insight into a work that had been previously been completely unknown. Barbara Giles joined the Land Army when she was 17 and believes that she not only gained independence but also greater understanding:

> It's nice that people are interested in the Land Army. My sister, my mother's younger sister and myself all went into the Land Army at Nightingale Farm, three of us on motorbikes and sidecars delivering milk all round the area. We took the jobs from the men to let them go into the forces, it made you more independent, and more self-assured. I can talk to anybody. Going round to customers, we got to know people, people who were hard up, in poverty, and it made you more sympathetic. It changed the face of the war when the Land Army took over.

For Helen Dawson, being in the Land Army was an immensely important experience. Still living in Bodiam, she has a painting of a land girl on her sitting room wall, which her children gave to her for her 80th birthday:

> I liked it. I liked the open-air life. People realized afterwards that if it wasn't for us, we were supplying the food, everything. It must have changed people's lives, especially the town girls; some of them had never seen a cow before. It has a special place. I got talking to someone and we talked about the war and she asked me what I did and I said, 'I was in the Land Army', and she said, 'So was I' and we're friends now and we meet up every so often.

The friend that Helen referred to was Eileen Hodd; she believes that women who served in the Land Army are bonded in a special way:

> I enjoyed that part of my life. It was hard, of course it was, [but] I loved it. I'm a country girl; you can see that by my garden now. We've been going to a lunch in the village and so does Helen [Dawson]. We never knew each other until two or three years ago. We started going to this lunch in the village and she sat beside me and we started chatting and we spoke and she said, 'I was in the Land Army' and I said, 'So was I'. So of course we shook hands and we were bonded for life then.

Eileen, like many other women, continued working in the Land Army after the war but left when she became pregnant. Widowed only three months into her marriage, she returned to work on the land after her son was born and continued doing so when she re-married.

Sheelah Cruttenden's children believe that it was her time in the Land Army that made their mother the woman she was. It was enormously important to her and she continued working in farming whenever possible:

> It made her what she came out to be in terms of jobs. She always worked on the land after that. She enjoyed it so much; she loved being outdoors. She did all sorts of jobs, she worked in M&S and as a dinner lady in the school but she worked at Merricks Farm in Icklesham apple picking, strawberries, apple sorting, pruning, hop training. Mum always used to sing: 'She'll be coming round the mountain when she comes, she'll be wearing a bonnet with WLA on it'.

Margaret Donaldson spent two years in the Land Army before leaving to join the ATS, which had been her first wish. Even so, she remembers her time in the Land Army with great affection and believes it broadened her horizons:

> I loved it. I enjoyed it very much. I loved the outdoor work even in the winter when we had to go down to cut the

mangolds. It was a frosty morning and I saw them all rolling their sleeves up, so I did the same and we just put the mangel-wurzels one side and the tops the other, and by the time I got to the end of the row, I was absolutely tingling with warmth. I was proud and the farmer must have been pleased with me because one day he said to me, 'Margaret you can take old Dobbin, or whatever his name was, down to the blacksmiths', and that was a great adventure and I just sat on old Dobbin and I rode him and I took my sweet rations down and while he was being shod, I went in and bought my sweet ration. That was lovely, a real adventure for a couple of hours just before the milking. I remember how kind they were to me, and the work itself. I remember the milking and the sterilization and working in the fields was great. It broadened my horizons. I learned quite a lot really, it was the first time I had been away from home so I learned how to live with other people and mix a bit better.

Pride in the Work

Whether they received official recognition or not, former land girls are proud of their achievements, and so they should be. Now aged 87, Phyllis Cole revisits Uckfield regularly, which is where she worked in a mobile threshing gang. For her the satisfaction was of a job well done:

The harvest wouldn't have been done would it? That satisfied us because we thought we were feeding people because the men had gone. We were aware of it at the time. I loved the countryside and I loved the welcome when you went in the village pub and going back afterwards and remembering, 'Oh, I was in that field'. There's a tearoom half way down Uckfield High Street and we get a wonderful welcome. We very often go back.

Hazel King is now 83, and has a large family: four daughters, one of whom died, ten grandchildren, six great grandchildren, and one great great grandchild. She often tells them about her life as a land girl and remains immensely proud of the work she did:

Some left straight away because we had married girls and gradually they all left and some went away to work. I stayed on until 1947. I got married in April '46 and worked up to the winter of '47 just before Christmas it was, and by that time I was pregnant so that's when I left. Mind you, I didn't like leaving. After I had my children I used to go out and work on the land. There was always plenty of work; potato picking, hop picking, fruit picking; there was always work for women. I wouldn't have changed it. It was a bit scary at times in the hit and run raids, but I wouldn't have changed it. We were happy, we use to sing on our way to work, you could always hear someone singing on the tractors and we got so good. If we had two or three working in the field, which most times there were because they were big fields, you could see we were singing and if we did the actions of the song, the other one would pick it up. I remember one song was *Coming in on a Wing and a Prayer*, and a lot of popular songs, wartime songs, it was good. We had to bring our tractors from Northiam down to Rye and that was the only time we were ever on the road. I wanted to show off. I'm a land girl and I'm driving a tractor. I was very proud of what I did. I'd still be there now if I wasn't married and had a family. We were given our jobs and we were expected to do them. There wasn't anything we didn't know about a tractor. It was a very good life and I dare anyone to say it wasn't.

Beryl Peacham, now in her 80s, still runs a smallholding, drives a combine harvester, and over winters sheep. She attends all the local Land Army reunions, and remembers her work as a land girl with immense pride.

Many women did not want to leave when the time came. Blanche Lucas, who lives in Etchingham, was one of them and remembers that the post-war adjustment could be difficult:

Well it was just something you accepted, going back to the life you'd had previously. I suppose up to a point it was a good feeling but then you'd miss it. Yes, I did miss it and to be honest, I would quite happily have gone on another few years and if it happened, I would be quite happy to play my part all over again. I was happy doing what I was doing and I was accepted. I did my work and we enjoyed ourselves. I suppose you could say we made the best of a bad job. Life is what you make it and we made it good, we made it pleasant on the whole in spite of the hard work and long hours and the only thing is we did get rather muscular. We did have a rather a nice badge to wear on our hats, we had these quite smart hats, felt hats, and they did look nice. I wish I'd saved my uniform. It was plodding and endurance, because we did plod and you endured it. I don't know whether the other services would have explained their jobs the same way as that: plodding and endurance rather than heroics…if you were a country girl you were at an advantage. It was harder for a town girl. I still like the outdoor life, I'd rather be outside than in, I still like it.

Liberating Women

None of the women interviewed for this book actually described themselves as feminists, which is not surprising for that era. However, none were in any doubt that they had all taken on what was seen as a male role and fulfilled it just as well as any man could have done. When asked, most women took this achievement as a matter of course but there were some, such as Joan Markby, 85, who felt the experience must have had a liberating impact on women's lives. For Joan, who left the Land Army in 1945, one of the most liberating aspects was, on reflection:

Getting out and doing what I had wanted to do, being outside. It's a beautiful part of the country down there [Dorset] and people were nice. I never went back to being a secretary. I stayed in farming until we got old and then we had a shop in Rye because you couldn't get any more land. We opened up a pottery. I loved driving a tractor. I see them go by because I can't drive a car with all this traffic. I'd love to be on a tractor saying, 'Here I am'. It certainly liberalized women.

It is difficult to assess the long-term impact of the Land Army. It is not difficult to assess its importance during the Second World War. In Barbara Giles' view, 'It changed the face of the war when the Land Army took over' and there can be no doubt that without the Land Army, British wartime food production would have suffered dreadful consequences. Women worked largely by hand but also learned to work changing technology and, when men returned to the land, it was land girls who showed them some of the new equipment and taught them how to use it. Inexperienced young women discovered potential and abilities within themselves that they did not know they possessed, and that is not knowledge that disappears and is reflected in the continuing self assurance of former land girls. How much their achievements impacted on the next generation of young women is very difficult to judge but it was the next generation that stood up and demanded greater rights for women, so perhaps that independence and pride was handed down.

> We were given our jobs and we were expected to do them. There wasn't anything we didn't know about a tractor. They were so basic, just sparking plugs and things like that. It was a very good life and I dare anyone to say it wasn't really. I often tell them [my children] about my life in the Land Army.
>
> (Hazel King)

Cows and Culture

Some land girls and timber workers reflected on their experiences through poetry. By and large, when most people think of war poets, it is the poetry of the First World War that comes to mind, particularly that of men such as Wilfred Owen. But women, too, recorded their thoughts on war through poetry, although much of it is often neglected. When Margaret Pyke wrote her final editorial for the *Land Girl* magazine in March 1947, she reminisced on the wealth of material that land girls had sent in to the magazine, commenting on the 'poems, articles, stories and drawings published in the magazine over the last seven years', which, in her opinion, proved that 'there was no reason whatever why cows and culture should not go together…'.

Certainly every month, the *Land Girl* contained poems written by land girls and timber workers. Some were humorous observations on the clothing. One appeared in February 1942 and was written by M.W. Phillips, a land girl in West Sussex, in the form of a rhyming letter addressed to the West Sussex County Secretary. It gives a clear idea of some of the problems around clothing, and the issues that county secretaries were tackling:

> Miss Adam, dear madam
> It is with regret
> I have to inform you
> I'm not fitted yet.
> The pullover's splendid
> And so is the mac
> And thanks for providing
> Two shirts for my back.
> The hat's on the large side
> But don't send another,
> I never wear hats
> So I've lent it to mother.
> The overall trousers
> Are roomy and rather
> Too long in the leg,
> But they're just right for father.
> I have three pairs of hose,
> And I thank you for sending 'em.
> (Good idea to enclose
> Some worsted for mending 'em).
> And now I must mention
> An article which is
> Requiring attention,
> My corduroy breeches.
> They are large round the waist,
> Though my hips try to stop 'em,
> I'm afraid they'll slip down,
> So please will you swap 'em.
> Believe me, Dear Madam,
> I'm sorry to trouble you.

Others bemoaned the impact of 'mucky' work on femininity, such as this poem called *Temporary Eclipse*, from March 1942, by Mary Cass, which also appeared in *Woman* magazine:

> Oh, how I'd love to be feminine and frail,
> With ten or twenty ardent suitors tagging at my tail,
> But my nose is such a shine
> As I shoo the hens to dine
> And scrub down the mucky kine,
> I'm a Land Girl.
>
> Oh, how I'd love to see a saucy Paris hat
> Perched on my well-groomed curls – just like that.
> But my breeches lack a crease,
> And my glamour's out on lease
> Till the day they sign the Peace.
> I'm a Land Girl.

War, Love and Philosophy

Other poems were more reflective, and focused on love, war and the countryside. In 1945 Vita Sackville-West put together a selection of poems written by land girls, which was published as *An Anthology of Verse* by members of the Women's Land Army. Most of the poems had already appeared in the *Land Girl* magazine but also in journals such as *Poetry Review, Country Life, Outposts,* and the *Children's Newspaper.* The anthology was reprinted by the Imperial War Museum in 1997, together with Vita Sackville-West's *The Women's Land Army.*

In her foreword to the anthology, Vita Sackville-West commented on the high standard of the poems, which she described as 'the talent concealed within the green jersey' and how one might have expected them to fall into just two categories, Humour and Nature, but that, in fact, although these categories were included, the poems also covered a wider range – 'war, love...[and] a more general philosophical spirit'. Interestingly, she was struck by the fact that they were free not just of sentimentality but also references to fluffy little lambs or newborn chicks. They also made no reference to machinery.

The poems in the *Anthology* are, as Vita Sackville-West

described, 'simple, straightforward and lovely'. Some reflect on the beauty of nature: one thing that seems to have united land girls, whether from town or country, was a deep love of the country itself. Those who came from the country already understood country ways and country life, but all evidence seems to suggest that women who came from the towns also developed a deep love of the countryside and missed it deeply if, and when, they returned to urban life.

Some of the poems, such as *Undowered* by Audrey Hancock seem to show that, although land girls did not receive formal gratuities, they felt themselves to be rich in other areas:

> Mine is the moonlight-silvered winding river,
> Mine are the trees that grow, the birds that sing,
> Mine are the happy woods, the friendly wild-flowers -
> For, having nothing, I have everything.
>
> Mine is the splendid sun, my bridge the rainbow,
> Mine are the shining darts the rain-clouds fling.
> Mine are the winding lanes, the curving hillsides –
> For, having nothing, I have everything.
>
> The boist'rous wind is my familiar playmate,
> The beauty that dawns and sunsets bring,
> The chattering streams are mine, and I am happy -
> For, having nothing, I have everything.

In her poem *War, Which Has Brought to Others Fear* Hebe Jerrold, who worked with the Women's Timber Corps, expressed what she had gained from her wartime experiences on the land, even if she felt slightly guilty about it:

> War, which has brought to others fear,
> Pain, sorrow, slavery and death,
> To me has brought what I hold dear
> And longed for but could not possess.
> Has given me wide stretch of sky,
> The sailing clouds, the wind's sharp breath,
> A roof of leaves, the wild flower's eye,
> Bird song, deep content and faith
> That at its source our stream runs clear.
> What have I done? I never meant
> To be a war-time profiteer!

The Fight Goes On

Some former members of the WLA and the Women's Timber Corps continued to campaign for recognition, and by the late 1990s there were signs that the British Government was starting to officially acknowledge the impact of the work of the WLA, a recognition that was long overdue. In January 1999, Mrs Jean Proctor, chair of the Land Army Association received an MBE for her services to the WLA, and the *Bolton News* reported on a local woman's two-year battle to win formal recognition and veteran status. In 2000 the British Government finally invited the WLA to join the Remembrance Day march past at the Cenotaph. In October 2007 the first monument to thousands of lumber jills who worked in the forests of Scotland was unveiled and will stand on a ridge in the Queen Elizabeth Forest in Aberfoyle. A former timber worker, now aged 81, who worked alongside Canadians, and married a Canadian, said that the timber workers had never been given the status of veterans and welcomed this belated memorial.

Former members of the Land Army continued to lobby for a formal medal to acknowledge their service, and politicians from all three parties pledged their support. One former land girl, Mildred Bowden, 87, from Tenterden, Kent, now leader of the Women's Land Army and Timber Corps Veteran group was quoted in the *Daily Telegraph* as saying: 'The country has never recognized our contribution. It hasn't said thank you to us.' The Land Army campaign was boosted by the Government's decision to award medals to thousands of 'Bevin Boys'; young men who were conscripted to work in the coal mines during the war and Hilary Benn, Secretary of State, asked civil servants to work on ways of recognizing the Land Army, saying, 'The Government is aware of the tremendous debt which the nation owes to the...Women's Land Army'. In December 2007, it was announced that after all these years and a long, hard struggle, surviving land girls were to receive a commendation in the form of a special badge. The first awards were made in January 2008.

Awards and medals

During the war individual Land Army members received awards, including 17 year old land girl, Grace Harrison, who worked in Kent and in 1942 received the British Empire Medal for bravery under fire; Mrs Simpson, Organizing Secretary, Northamptonshire who received an MBE in 1944 and Misses Bedford (Cornwall), Birtwistle (Wiltshire) and Laycock (Denbighshire) who received the British Empire Medal also in 1944. Lady Denman was awarded an MBE in 1946, and in 1999 Mrs Jean Proctor, chair of the Land Army Association was awarded an MBE.

Bibliography and Further Reading

Specific

Hall, Annie, *Land Girl*, Ex Libris Press, 1993

Huxley,Gervais, *Lady Denman, G.B.E.*, Chatto & Windus, 1961

Knighton, Joyce, *Land Army Days: Cinderellas of the Soil*, Aurora Publishing, 1994

Sackville-West, Vita, *The Women's Land Army*, Michael Joseph, 1944, reprinted Imperial War Museum, 1997

Tyrer, Nicola, *They Fought in the Fields*, Mandarin Paperbacks, 1997

An Anthology of Verse by members of the Women's Land Army first published c.1945, reprinted 1997, Imperial War Museum

Meet the Members: A Record of the Timber Corps of the Women's Land Army, first published c.1945, reprinted 1997, Imperial War Museum

The *Land Girl* 1940-1950, magazine of the Women's Land Army

The *Landswoman* 1918-20, magazine of the Women's Land Army

The *Sussex Express and County Herald* (selected issues covering 1939-45)

General

Adie, Kate, *Corsets to Camouflage: Women and War*, Hodder & Stoughton, 2003

Braybon, Gail & Summerfield, Penny, *Out of the Cage: Women's Experiences in Two World Wars*, Pandora Press, 1987

Fountain, Nigel, consulting editor, *Women at War: Voices from the Twentieth Century from the Imperial War Museum*, Michael O'Mara Books Ltd, 2002, includes CD

Gardiner, Juliet, *Wartime Britain 1939-1945*, Headline Book Publishing, 2005

Goodall, Felicity, *Voices from the Home Front: Personal Experiences of Wartime Britain 1939-45*, David & Charles, 2004

Harris, Carol, *Women at War 1939-1945: The Home Front*, Sutton Publishing, 2000

Marlow, Joyce, ed., *The Virago Book of Women and the Great War*, Virago Press, 1998
Nicholson, Mavis, *What Did You Do in the War, Mummy?*, Chatto & Windus, 1995
Sheridan, Dorothy, ed.,*Wartime Women: A Mass Observation Anthology 1937-45*, Phoenix Press, 1990

Oxford Dictionary of National Biography
The Times (Digital Archive)

Websites
http://www.bbc.co.uk/ww2peopleswar/

Includes personal accounts from women who served in the Women's Land Army and Women's Timber Corps.

www.landarmy.org.uk

Oral accounts on DVD plus study pack for teachers on the Women's Land Army and Timber Corps. DVD available through Quiet Hero Productions. See site.

Museums
Brenzett Aeronautical Museum, Brenzett, Romney Marsh, Kent. Formerly a Woman's Land Army hostel, includes a permanent exhibition on the WLA. Open to visit from Easter – end October, weekends.

Imperial War Museum, London
Holds archived material about the WLA and a permanent exhibition.

The Museum of English Rural Life, University of Reading, Reading

Women's Land Army Museum, Dover, Kent

Index

accidents and injuries, 72-3
Agricultural Wages Act, 1924, 11
air raids, 73-6
A Land Girl's Memories, 27
American soldiers, 143-4
American Women's Land Army, 95
Appeal for Women Land Workers, 1916, 3
Australian Women's Land Army (AWLA), 94-5
Auxiliary Territorial Service (ATS), 14
Awards, 165, 176, 177

Back to the Land, 12
Balcombe Place, Sussex, 17-19
'Battle for Wheat', 12
Beaverbrook, Lord, 31
Benn, Hilary, 176
Beveridge, Sir William, 10
Bevin, Ernest, 31, 36, 152, 153, 157
billets, 97-103
  complaints about 102ff
Birch, Bernice, 50, 104
Blythe, Aubrey, 111, 148
bombs and doodlebugs, 72-6
Bowden, Mildred, 176
boyfriends, 138-40
Brenzett WLA Hostel, 108
Brignall, Ray, 108

certificates, leaving, 160, 161
Churchill, Winston, 152, 157
Cole, Phyllis, 43, 47, 65-6, 103-4, 122, 130, 140-1, 169
conscription, women, Second World War, 35-7
County committees, WLA, 19, 164
cruelty, 125
Cruttenden, Sheelah, 39, 109-11, 138, 144-5, 158

Daily Express, 31
Dawson, Helen, 41, 44, 46, 49, 61-2, 97, 140, 167
de la Warr, Diana Countess, 24, 29
Denman, Lady Gertrude, 5, 15-18, 19-21, 22-3, 48
  appointed WLA director, 17
  awarded Grand Cross of British Empire, 164
  challenging discrimination, 132, 151-2
  improves wages and condi tions, 76-7, 78, 132
  resigns from WLA, 153-6
  urging support, 32-3
discrimination, against Land Girls, 131-3
Donaldson, Margaret, 45, 54-5, 62-3, 66-7, 71, 99, 168
doodlebugs, 74
Dumbleton Hall, 109-10, 138

Emergency Powers Act, The, 1939, 11
entertainment, 140-5
Essential Work Order (EWO), 36

farmers,
    negative attitudes, 29-31ff, 119
    positive attitudes, 127-9
farming, British
    increased production, 55
    on eve of Second World War, 10-11
    primitive conditions, 70
fitting into country life, 119-21
food, 101-2
food production, 55, 150

Gibbs, Annice, timber worker, 83-4
Giles, Barbara, 43-4, 63-4, 146, 167, 172
Gloucestershire Echo, 158, 159
Goodhart, Anstace, timber worker, 88-9
Grabham, Eileen, 39-40, 47, 96-7, 145, 148, 153

Hale, Kathleen, 6
Hastings Observer, 38
health checks, 39, 51
Hignett, Rose, 153
hit and run raids, 74
Hodd, Eileen, 38, 43, 45, 50, 77-8, 112, 141-2, 153
Holness, Arthur, 129-30
Hope, Stella, 40-1, 114-18, 163-4
hostels, 108-11
hours of work, 76-7, 78
Hudson, Robert, 32, 35, 152, 153

isolation and loneliness, 104-6

Jenkins, Mrs Inez, 17, 154
jokes and ridicule, 54-5

King, Hazel, 42, 46-7, 67-9, 74, 101-2, 103, 112-13, 135, 139-40, 169-70

Land Army see Women's Land Army

Land Girl, The, 18, 35, 51, 105-6, 132
    advice to Land Girls, 51, 60-1
    advice to town girls, 119-21
    ceases publication, 163
    final editorial, 172-3
    on cosmetics, 120-1
    on Lady Denman's resignation, 155
    on wearing hats correctly, 146-7
Land Army Manual, 18, 59, 107
Land Girls,
    admiration for, 126-30, 150
    ages, 44-5
    appeals for, 24, 29, 37
    as second-class citizens, 132
    bravery under fire, 74-5
    civilian status, 20, 44
    class, 42
    discrimination against, 131-3
    excluded from post-war benefits, 152-3
    isolation, 104-6
    lack of experience, 51-4
    previous occupations, 43-4
    pride in work, 79
    protest lack of recognition, 157-9
    recruitment, 24-34
    reflections on war work, 166-72
    social backgrounds, 42-7
    time off, 136-46
    views about uniform, 48-50, 148
    working conditions, 76-9
    working with POWs, 111-13
    see also Women's Land Army
Landswoman, The, 6, 7, 8
Land Worker, 31
lavatories, lack of, 103-4
leaving home, 45-6, 96-7

Lloyd George, David, 6
Lucas, Blanche, 46, 49-50, 53, 56-7, 72-3, 121, 144, 170-1
Lumber jills *see* Women's Timber Corps

Markby, Joan, 43, 53, 64-5, 100, 165, 171
marriage, 145-6
McDowell, Pamela, 55, 99, 123-4, 131
Meet the Members, 92, 129
Merrit, June Ivy, 109
milking and dairy work, 62-3
Ministry of Agriculture, 15, 16,

National Farmers' Union (NFU), 11, 156, 164
National Union of Agricultural Workers, 30, 129-30, 158

opposition to women workers, 28, 29

Parker, Pat, timber worker, 84-5, 86-8, 101, 135,
Peacham, Beryl, 12, 51-2, 75-6, 97, 124-5, 142-3, 170
Pearce, Peggy, 26, 48-9, 65, 69-70, 98, 100, 107, 125 136
Picture Post, 32, 34-5
'ploughing up' campaign, 12
poetry, 172-5
post-war choices for Land Girls, 162-3
post-war retraining, land girls excluded, 151
pregnancies and abortions, 136
prisoners of war (POWs), 111-13
prejudice (against Land Girls), 119-33
   from farmers, 29-31, 119, 122, 123,
   from other forces' women, 132-3, 143
   from the public, 90, 130
   overcoming prejudice, 34, 126, 126-7, 130ff

Pyke, Mrs Margaret, 18, 105, 146-7, 149, 153, 161
Queen Elizabeth, the Queen Mother, thanks to Land Army, 160-1
rape, 126
rat catching, 71-2
rationing, water, 99
recruitment,
   First World War, 3, 5-7
   interviews, 40
   offices, 25
   posters and propaganda, 38-9
   rallies, 38
   Second World War, 24-34, 199
   starts again, 149
Reinstatement in Civil Employment Act (1944), 151-2
Roosevelt, Eleanor, 95
Royal Patronage, 21
Sackville-West, Vita, 15, 19, 43, 53
   on county reps, 107
   on timber workers, 85, 91, 93
   on uniform and land girls, 147-8
sexism, 29, 123-5, 134-6
sexual harassment, 123, 124, 125-6
Smith, Mr Dorman, 16-17
strikes and protests, 157-9
Summerskill, Edith, 36-7, 157
Sussex Express and County Herald, 24, 35, 72, 102, 128-9, 156
Talbot, Dame Meriel, 1, 2, 3, 4, 5, 33-4
Temporary Eclipse (poem), 174
The Land Girls (1998), 135
They Fought in the Fields, 152
threshing, 66, 70
time off, 136-46
To All Land Girls, 52

tractor driving, 67-9
training, 27-8, 60-3
   lack of, 51-2
trade unions, changing attitudes,
   129-30
tributes, 126-7, 129
Undowered (poem), 175
uniform,
   First World War, 8
   rules about, 146-8
   Women's Land Army, 8, 48-
      51ff
   women's thoughts about,
      48-51, 145, 146-8
   Women's Timber Corps, 82
victory parades, 161-2
wage boards, 11
wages and conditions, 76-7
   compared with other
      forces'women, 131-3
War Ag *see* War Agricultural
   Committees
War Agricultural Committees
   (War Ags), 11, 13
Ward, Irene, 37
War, Which Has Brought to Others
   Fear (poem), 175
welfare, 106-8
Williams, Mrs Rowland, 4
women,
   employment 1939, 14
   life on eve of Second World
      War, 13-14
   response to war, 36
   war work, 36-7
Women's Agricultural
   Committees, 5
Women's Consultative
   Committee, 36
Women's Defence Relief Corps, 3
Women's Farm and Garden
   Association, 1, 3, 4
Women's Forestry Corps, 7
Women's Land Army,

achievements, 164
administration, 20
class differences and
   tensions, 20, 107, 121
county representatives
   (reps), 106
First World War, 1-9
headquarters, 17-19
lack of recognition, 151ff
official song, 12
origins of, 1-2
post-war need for, 150-1
reasons for joining, 44-8
reformed 1939, 17
Second World War, 17, 18ff
stands down, 164
status, 21
survey of work during First
   World War, 9
welfare, 106-7
Women's Land Army Benevolent
   Fund, 132
Women's Land Army, The 18, 53
   description of Balcombe
      Place, 18
   overview of Land Girls'
      work, 59
Women's League, 3
Women's National Land Service
   Corps, 4,
Women's Timber Corps, 58, 80-95
   disbanded, 163
   monument to, 176
   pole selecting, 88-90
   sawmills, 93
   training, 83-5
   tree felling, 92-3
   types of work, 85-6
Women's Voluntary Services for
   Air Raid Precautions
   (WVS), 14
work on the land, 58-79ff
   during bombing raids, 72-6
   types of work, 58-60
   with animals, 69-70